philosophies of
EDUCATION

philosophies of
EDUCATION

edited by PHILIP H. PHENIX

Sketches of some contemporary viewpoints on education based on a series of educational television programs produced by KTCA-TV (Minneapolis-St. Paul) for the National Educational Television and Radio Center

John Wiley & Sons, Inc.
New York • London • Sydney

20 19 18 17 16 15 14 13 12 11

ISBN 0 471 68640 9

Library of Congress Catalog Card Number: 61-11178

Printed in the United States of America

CONTENTS

· Introduction

Philip H. Phenix

• "It is clear that there should be legislation about education and that it should be conducted on a public system. But consideration must be given to the question, what constitutes education and what is the proper way to be educated. At present there are differences of opinion as to the proper tasks to be set; for all peoples do not agree as to the things that the young ought to learn, either with a view to virtue or with a view to the best life, nor is it clear whether their studies should be regulated more with regard to intellect or with regard to character. And confusing questions arise out of the education that actually prevails, and it is not at all clear whether the pupils should practice pursuits that are practically useful, or morally edifying, or higher accomplishments—for all these views have won the support of some judges; and nothing is agreed as regards the exercise conducive to virtue, for, to start with, all men do not honor the same virtue, so that they naturally hold different opinions in regard to training in virtue."

ARISTOTLE: *Politics* VIII.2

There is widespread concern among Americans today about education. The rapid changes in modern life impose new conditions with which all citizens—young and old—must learn how to deal. The slower pace of earlier ages made the tasks of education far simpler than they are now, for there was a reasonably stable body of knowledge, skill, custom, and tradition which formed the material of instruction. In the past few decades all that made for security and continuity seems to have been shattered. Knowledge is multiplying far beyond the limits of general comprehension. The proliferation of new techniques is making even recently acquired skills obsolescent. Inherited modes of thought and conduct have been displaced or are under challenge. Mighty political, economic, and social convulsions are shaking the nations of the world, and militant new ideologies are offered for the salvation of men's souls.

In such a time it is little wonder that education is under fresh scrutiny. We want to know what aspects of past education have contributed to our present difficulties and what aspects have provided resources to meet them. Faced with a superabundance of things to be learned, we want to be able to choose the most important ones. We are searching for standards by which to distinguish essential from nonessential elements in the curriculum and desirable from undesirable kinds of instruction.

The problems of education are not presented to school teachers and administrators alone. Students and parents are also faced with them directly; but then so are all citizens in a democracy. Although the supervision of American education is ultimately the responsibility of the several states, we have long-established traditions of local control. Despite the recent growth in Federal responsibility for certain aspects of education, wide diffusion of authority has been the rule. Parents are granted freedom in choice of schools for their children, and great variations in school practice, in both public and non-public institutions, are permitted. It follows that to a large extent individual citizens can have an effective voice in educational affairs. The large issues to be decided are not merely for professionals or for big government; they are everyone's responsibility.

There are, of course, many decisions about teaching and learning which should be left to professionally trained people. Laymen cannot generally be expected to have the knowledge and experience necessary to make wise choices in such matters as the best teaching materials in mathematics or the proper equipping of classrooms—although keen lay judgment sometimes surpasses the experts' wisdom even in these technical questions. The decisions which should not be referred to professional educators are those relating to the aims of education— the ends toward which teaching and learning are expected to contribute.

Differences in educational practice—in courses of study, teaching methods, administrative procedures, and patterns of support and control—are generally reflections of differing beliefs about such matters as human nature, knowledge, values, and the good society. These beliefs are the foundation of differing *philosophies of education.* A "philosophy of education" is any reasonably coherent set of values and fundamental assumptions used as a basis for evaluating and guiding educational practice.

Decisions about education can best be made intelligently and consistently in the light of a mature and reflective philosophy of education. Citizens cannot wisely discharge their educational responsibilities if they attempt to deal with separate issues piecemeal and without any broad frame of reference. Thus, educational philosophy is pertinent to everyone. It is not necessarily an abstruse technical discipline open only to those trained in the field, although there is such a specialty and there are experts in it. Every person who has a reflectively-held point of view about basic values and assumptions in education has a philosophy of education.

It is important that discussions of education in these critical times be carried on in the light of the philosophic issues involved. At any more superficial level, the true causes of disagreement will not be discerned. The current debates about education provide an unparalleled oportunity to take stock of ourselves, as individuals and as a society, in respect to the values by which we live and our guiding convictions about man and the world, the sources from which they spring, and the destiny toward which they tend.

The present volume is offered as a modest contribution to the encouragement of philosophic reflection on educational issues by the concerned lay public. Thirteen leaders in education set forth here some of the main ideas in their respective philosophies of education. These statements were originally presented on a series of filmed television programs produced by KTCA-TV, (Minneapolis-St. Paul), the Twin City Area Educational Television Corporation, for the National

Educational Television and Radio Center, for distribution to Educational Television stations throughout the country. Limitations of time and considerations of simplicity under broadcast conditions made it impossible for the speakers to cover their subjects with any degree of thoroughness or to do more than suggest the major principles of their respective viewpoints. The successive chapters in this book contain the substance of the broadcast programs, with minor modifications required by the change from screen to printed page.

Readers who are also viewers of the television series will be aware of one basic difference in format, which should be acknowledged here. On the television series, each guest speaker was introduced and interrogated by Dr. Harvey M. Rice, President of Macalester College in St. Paul, Minnesota. In the book no host is required, and so Dr. Rice does not appear elsewhere in its pages. Nonetheless, the reader may wish to know that it was Dr. Rice who served on the televised programs much as the editor serves this book.

For each of the philosophies of education an introductory paragraph by the editor is provided at the beginning of the chapter in order to put each position in historical perspective. Following this is a representative quotation which briefly epitomizes the viewpoint. Then comes the exponent's viewpoint statement, succeeded by his answers to typical objections raised by critics of the position. Next, for purposes of illustration, a concrete educational situation is described, and the author's reactions to it in the light of his viewpoint are stated. Finally, each chapter is concluded with a few suggestions as to what parents, teachers, school board members, and other concerned citizens should do in order to put that particular philosophy into effect.

The philosophies treated in the following chapters do not by any means exhaust the field. A great many other systems of value and belief could have been chosen instead. The thirteen included are, however, representative of the main varieties of positions from which educational policy making in America proceeds.

Only two of the positions are philosophies in the technical sense. These are Experimentalism and Classical Realism. Three of the viewpoints grow out of and represent the three major religious traditions in the United States. The other eight positions are organized around certain values and attitudes which have resulted in characteristic and widely-advocated proposals for education.

The authors are all recognized as authoritative spokesman for the philosophies of education they represent. However, most of them are not professional philosophers of education, just as the positions they present are not for the most part philosophies in the technical sense. Hullfish, Broudy, Henle, and Brameld can all be classified as professional philosophers of education. Stratemeyer is a curriculum specialist, Bestor is a historian, Jersild and Ligon are psychologists, Cuninggim is an educational administrator and foundation executive, Borowitz is a specialist in religious education, Kirk is an author, editor, and social critic, Stoke is a political scientist and administrator, and Butts is a historian of education. Despite this variety of professional specialties, each of the authors has become a leading exponent of a distinctive viewpoint which is sufficiently reflective and fundamental to be designated in the broad sense as a philosophy of education.

The logic of arrangement for the chapters is as follows: The first two chapters present the main two basic philosophic orientations, Experimentalism and Classical Realism. The next four represent views of education which center around the individual—Life Adjustment and Psychological Maturity are akin to Experimentalism, and Intellectual Discipline and Moral Character belong more to the Classical Realism tradition. The last four chapters represent dominantly social rather than individual emphases, with Reconstructionism and Freedom (which follow in the Experimentalist line) ranged opposite Conservatism and National Survival (which are generally in the Classical Realist line). The three religious views occupy a position intermediate between the individual and social emphases. With such an arrangement, an alternation of what may very roughly be called "liberal" and "conservative" viewpoints is secured. In this way, a reading of the chapters in their given order should provide a good sense of the major contrasting outlooks in education today and of the differing values and beliefs which underlie educational issues.

It is hoped that out of participation in what is thus in effect a dialogue the reader may find help in the clarification of his own ideas about education, so that he may better exercise his responsibility as a citizen in these exacting times.

Two final words need to be added. First, readers must bear in mind the circumstances under which these sketches of the various positions were presented, namely, as brief television programs on which only a few points could be made, without any opportunity for adequate or well-documented development. The authors are well aware of the limitations of their materials, and have granted permission to have them presented in the present book with the understanding that the informal and limited nature of the discussions would be clearly explained to the readers.

The second is a word of acknowledgment. The impetus and encouragement for undertaking this volume to serve as a companion to the broadcast programs are due to Dr. John Schwarzwalder, General Manager of KTCA-TV, the Twin City Area Educational Television Corporation. Thanks are also due to Mr. Joseph T. McDermott, Special Projects Director for KTCA-TV, who worked closely with the editor in preparing the television programs and who gave valuable assistance in the compiling of the materials for the book. Finally, credit goes to Mrs. Harriet Soll for writing some of the materials used in the illustrative examples.

CHAPTER 1 · An Experimentalist
View of Education

H. Gordon Hullfish

• Experimentalism as an explicit and systematic theory
of education stems primarily from the work of John
Dewey. It belongs to the twentieth century, and,
like Dewey, it is characteristically American in its
temper and outlook.

Other American philosophers of Dewey's generation—notably Charles Sanders Peirce, George Her-
bert Mead, and William James—shared the same
fundamental outlook. All of these men were pro-
foundly concerned with modern science and with
its effects on our ways of thinking and acting.

Throughout the history of western civilization,
many educational thinkers have emphasized the
importance of experience, experimentation, and
learning by doing. We think of such diverse people
as the engineers of ancient Egypt, Aristotle as a
scientist, the architects who constructed the Roman
cities, the alchemists of the Middle Ages, the artist-
inventor Leonardo da Vinci, Galileo, Francis Bacon,
and a host of more recent figures. But experimentalism as a comprehensive philosophy had to
await the coming of modern science, technology, and
industrialism to be brought to full fruition.—EDITOR.

• *"It is not the business of the school to transport youth from an environment of activity into one of cramped study of the records of other
men's learning; but to transport them from an environment of relatively
chance activities, into one of activities selected with reference to guidance of learning. The most direct blow at the traditional separation
of doing and knowing and at the traditional prestige of purely "intellectual" studies has been given by the progress of experimental science.
If this progress has demonstrated anything, it is that there is no such
thing as genuine knowledge and fruitful understanding except as the
offspring of doing. Men have to do something to things when they
wish to find out something; they have to alter conditions. This is the
lesson of the laboratory method, and the lesson which all education
has to learn."* [1]

STATEMENT OF THE VIEWPOINT BY H. GORDON HULLFISH

As already suggested in the editor's note, the experimentalist turns *to* experience rather than *away* from it in order to find values that are to direct this experience. Obviously, anyone in the field of philosophy is looking for values to which he can give his allegiance and which, in his judgment, will provide direction for the life of man. Many have turned away from experience. Experimentalists on the contrary, turn to experience, believing that values emerge in the stresses and strains and in the hopes and aspirations of daily life and that these, when further reflected upon and refined, are then set up as ideals to serve until such time as it seems necessary for them to undergo reconstruction in order that they may guide human activities more effectively.

The experimentalist believes that intelligence, operating in quite human ways in relation to quite human problems, will give the answers that are needed to bring the newly born infant to maturity. At the onset of life the infant is totally helpless and it is within and through experience that he progresses into adulthood. The experimentalist believes also that the values which men have developed in their past are the values with which they must start at any given time. Because of this interrelationship of the individual and the transmitted culture, the experimentalist further affirms that the quality of the relationships in society will be reflected in the quality of the individual human experience. Thus, the experimentalist asks what kind of social structure, of social values, provides what is best for the most people. Here he turns to the heritage of democracy, with its faith in the capacities of human nature, in human intelligence, and in the fruits of cooperative experience.

Certain consequences of this position for education seem to me to be fairly obvious. The experimentalist wants an active school and an active student. He wants activity but not in order to glorify activity, which in itself may be aimless, as indeed experience itself may be miseducative. In the quotation at the beginning of the chapter, Dewey suggests that the business of education is to replace chance activity by *activity that leads to genuine knowledge and to fruitful understanding.* This means that the teacher cannot be happy just because there is activity in the classroom. He has the moral responsibility of organizing, selecting, and directing experiences so that participation in activities—whether in groups or on an individual basis —will bring a maximum of understanding and knowledge to the individual.

We should recognize, moreover, that interest is a critical factor in learning. But it is important in this connection to realize that the teacher has the responsibility of arousing interest, not merely of looking around to see if he can find it. This is one of the places where progressive education has been most misunderstood. So, while I am emphasizing interest, I am also stressing the obligation of the teacher for stimulating and directing interest.

I would also like to point out that we cannot carry on an activity within the present so that it leads to further knowledge and has the consequences of enlarging and deepening understanding, unless we make use of the knowledge that man has gained in the past. Here the important point for the experimentalist is that knowledge is not simply revered because it comes from the past; it is used to help young people solve the problems they now confront. Thus, the teacher has the responsibility of arousing interest so that young people will be led to knowledge that will help them deal with the problems they face now, and so that they may progressively organize more and more ranges of knowledge which will progressively operate more effectively for them.

I would add just this: in an experimentalist classroom, two things would be expected to predominate: The first of these may be called the "continuity of a reflective atmosphere," where students are not merely engaged in fruitless memorization but are thinking through problems of concern and are being helped to do so by the knowledge they bring to bear on them. The second expected thing, if we take seriously the development of the quality of human relationships, may be called the "continuity of a democratic atmosphere." In this young people will not merely acquire more and more knowledge, but will learn progressively how people who take democracy seriously should take other individuals seriously, so that the whole human enterprise may be improved. I do not wish to suggest for a moment that experimentalism is the only road to democracy, but I will say that it looks like the best bet to me.

Answers to Objections

Doesn't the teacher who follows the experimentalist point of view tend to emphasize the present and the future at the expense of the accumulated wisdom of mankind?

This is a fair question. It has been raised by a good many people. While many teachers, in fact, may do exactly what the question implies, theoretically the experimentalist position does not hold that the past may be neglected. What the position does suggest, as I have already pointed out, is that knowledge is not to be revered simply because it is of the past, but it should be respected exactly to the degree that it functions in a present situation to help young people understand the present and to shed light on the future. I see nothing in the point of view that gives any teacher the warrant to ignore the contributions of the past.

In our rapidly changing world is it not more important to give young people something to hold on to than merely teaching them to be concerned with today or tomorrow?

Very definitely. But look at that phrase, "something to hold on to." The really critical problem arises right here. It is possible to hold on to values which are given by some one in authority—a "mother knows best" approach to life. The one difficulty with this is that if anything goes wrong with the values thus given so that they do not apply today, it is necessary to look around for another authority. In the experimentalist view, we do not get security by values that have been handed to us. We gain personal security exactly to the degree that we develop a method of dealing with the problems we confront, so that we feel secure in our ability to get answers to problems and difficulties as these arise. We do not bring the answers out of the past and impose them on present problems. We bring such knowledge as we possess together with a method (a method of being intelligent in relation to current difficulties), to help find answers relevant to the present situations.

Has not progressive education, which is an outgrowth of experimentalism, failed to produce the capable and disciplined citizens that these exacting times require?

We have almost no evidence that makes it possible to give a clear answer to this question. Certainly, the progressive educators have been accused of so operating the school that undisciplined people emerge. Yet it is a fact that only a very small percentage of schools or of teachers in this country would call themselves progressive; and, even though schools have been influenced by the experimentalist point of view, they have not been so influenced that they are progressive in all respects. Our schools are a mixture of much that is new and much that is old. So it is very difficult to get evidence that would support the view taken in the question.

If experimentalism teaches that nothing is absolutely true or right, but that knowledge grows out of social situations and each individual's reaction to them, does not the position lead young people to assume that it is not necessary to take seriously anything they are taught?

The answer depends entirely on the quality of the classroom situation, the way in which those who teach deal with knowledge, with problems, and with students. The experimentalist position does not suggest that we may operate arbitrarily, ignoring the past. What it does suggest is that everything, including our values, our knowledge, and our experience, undergoes change. The problem then is whether we undergo change under completely haphazard conditions or under conditions directed by intelligence. Now to the degree that the experimentalist point of view does function within the school, young people are progressively learning to think better, and nothing is more disciplinary than the process of thinking itself. If a person engages in this process, he cannot take a casual attitude toward his beliefs. He takes them very seriously and accepts the responsibility for organizing the evidence to support them. If properly taught, young people in an experimentalist program will become quite responsible, because they know that they are personally involved in the securing of answers. It is not a question of accepting or not accepting what somebody else believes.

An Example for Illustration and Comment

(This is a scene from an eighth grade social studies classroom.)

The class is engaged in a project for the study of city government. Last week the students made a field trip to the local city hall to observe firsthand how their own city was governed. Now they have divided themselves into specific interest groups for the purpose of more intensive study on particular aspects of the topic. The teacher moves quietly from group to group, offering assistance where needed and making suggestions to advance the work of the committees.

Within each group there is appropriate division of labor. Some consult reference books, others prepare charts, still others analyze data and compile reports.

One group is delving into how the city can best be governed. They have collected data from cities using various plans, noting the success or failure in each. After weighing all the evidence, they will bring it to the entire class so a decision can be made on what form of government will best serve the theoretical model city they are building.

A second group is hard at work on the traffic problem. They have built a scale model of a proposed highway system, to demonstrate graphically the way in which existing traffic problems might be overcome.

A third group is concerned with community services, and has prepared a set of specifications for medical, recreational, and educational services in their city.

The room is a scene of quiet, coordinated activity. The students move about freely. They work at committee work tables, going and coming as necessary to consult reference books on the shelves or to secure construction materials, and talking with one another and with the teacher in pursuit of their plans.

In this example several things stand out. The students are learning from direct experience, and they are dealing with real problems which they are going to have to face as citizens. They are organized into interest groups, and we may suppose that the teacher deliberately presented suggestions to stimulate interest. The general social quality of the classroom also seems quite excellent. We cannot be sure of this from such a description, without actually being present, but apparently these young people are working well one with another and are going about their work in a reflective manner.

It is important also to note that, although the teacher is present and is being helpful at all points, he is not obtrusive. Yet I expect that this teacher is definitely in control of the situation. The example illustrates another basic point which is frequently overlooked. This situation is a disciplined situation. Youngsters are moving about freely, but in such a way as to advance the common enterprise and not to interfere with the work of others. It is too often thought that there is discipline only when young people are sitting quietly, and making no movement of any sort. I like the disciplined freedom of movement suggested by the example.

Concluding Suggestions

Parents and citizens must see to it that the schools have adequate financial support. It takes very good teachers to conduct a class of the kind just described—teachers who are not merely experts in a field of knowledge but who know something about the significance of this field for the social relationships within which the knowledge is to be used. For example, it does little good, it seems to me, to set up a project which gives youngsters only theoretical knowledge about how to plan a community. The significance comes in somehow translating what they learn into the life of the community itself.

Parents and other citizens can help by being sympathetic listeners to young people as they get excited and want to talk about their ideas. Adults should not say, "Those are problems that should not concern young people." Take, for instance, the matter of planning traffic in a community. It concerns today's young people very much. They themselves must use the streets as pedestrians, and soon, if not already, they will be using them as drivers of automobiles. So if anything can be done in a community to ease the traffic problem and to reduce the terrible loss of life and limb caused by automobile accidents, it will be a tremendous gain.

I am not suggesting that the school take the leadership in such social and civic improvement. I am saying that it is unfortunate if young people simply go through the motions in a classroom like the one described, so that what they learn is as abstract as anything they could learn from books.

Finally, parents should show concern about what the school is doing. They should not merely tolerate the school; they should give psychological support to teachers. They can help teachers move beyond the limitations of simple routinized memory work, in which youngsters may build a lasting dislike for education, and hence a lasting dislike for knowledge. One of the happy consequences of good teaching is that young people will come to see the difference that knowledge makes and, therefore, be receptive to it.

CHAPTER 2 · A Classical Realist
View of Education

Harry S. Broudy

• Classical realism is presented as a basic view contrasting with experimentalism, the philosophy examined in the first chapter. Experimentalism, concerned with the modern and the changing, is closely related to education for life adjustment, for psychological maturity, for cultural reconstruction, and for freedom —philosophies that will be treated in later chapters of this book. Classical realism, more concerned with established tradition, is closely related to education for intellectual discipline, for moral character, for cultural conservatism, and for national survival, as well as to the three major American religious philosophies of education—all of which will also be treated in later chapters.

Classical realism stems from ancient Greece, chiefly from Plato and Aristotle. It formed the basis for the great medieval systems of thought which culminated in that of Thomas Aquinas. It has come down to the present day in important segments of the literary, philosophic, and scientific movements.—EDITOR.

• *"The aim of education, as the realist sees it, is four-fold: to discern the truth about things as they really are and to extend and integrate such truth as is known; to gain such practical knowledge of life in general and of professional functions in particular as can be theoretically grounded and justified; and finally, to transmit this in a coherent and convincing way both to young and old throughout the human community.*

Education is the art of communicating truth. It has not been fully achieved until this truth not only lies within but actually possesses the mind and heart of the student. This process of communication is both theoretical and practical, but the theoretical is prior. The child, of course, should be interested in what he is learning. But it does not follow that whatever the child is interested in is, therefore, valuable. This is absurd. The skill of the teacher lies in eliciting the interests of the child in the right things, especially in grasping the truth for its own sake." [2]

STATEMENT OF THE VIEWPOINT BY HARRY S. BROUDY

Let me first explain why this position is referred to as "classical realism." In the first place, "classical" refers to something that happened a long time ago, and this position takes its departure from Aristotle and Plato, who lived a good long time ago. In the second place, something is called "classical" because it seems to mark a high peak of achievement in our cultural history, as, for example, in the field of philosophy. A "classical" epoch is a time when geniuses somehow have great insights into the meaning of human life and preserve these insights either in philosophy or in fine art or literature. These inherited treasures have been called "classical" ever since. It is for these reasons that the position is called *classical* realism.

The second word, "realism," is not so easy. Maybe I can get at it this way: Practically any object we look at or think about has a content and a form. A triangle can be made out of almost anything, but it always has a triangular form. A man has a form and he is made up of contents that are somehow shaped by that form. The ancients felt that to understand anything is to apprehend this form, which they called an "intelligible species." Plato taught that the form is the *real* part of the object. The real part of a chair is the form, or as we might say, the "formula" of the chair. Plato called these forms "ideas" and put them in a realm all their own. That is why his doctrine is called "Platonic realism."

In classical realism we retain this central principle that the forms of things are their most important parts. We hold that the way to know things is by apprehending their forms. But above all, we believe that the forms are *real*, that they are in objects. They are not put there by us, they are not figments of imagination, they are not the products of a culture, they are in things.

What does this view lead to? We take one further step and affirm that human life has a form. It has a law, a natural law. If we could apprehend this natural law, if we could only discern the form of human nature and the form of physical nature, we would have an insight into the goals and standards appropriate for the good life. That is why the classical realist, when he turns to education, tends to think of it as a means of getting the young, immature person to realize the form inherent in things—to realize his own form and thereby to achieve the good life for himself and mankind.

Let me turn now to what I regard as the major problem in education today, and indicate how the classical realist would solve it. It seems to me that our greatest problem is in what we call "general education." We mean by this term, on the one hand, studies which yield knowledge that will apply to a wide variety of situations—subjects like mathematics, science, or literature—because they are theoretical. In a democracy, on the other hand, we often mean by "general education" topics or skills that everybody in the school population can learn. Here is where the problem arises. If we choose a set of studies that will apply widely, the number of people who can learn them well is relatively small. If we teach what everyone can learn, the curriculum has little theoretical power. Thus we are in a dilemma. With one kind of curriculum we get generality of one kind; with another kind of curriculum we get generality of another kind. The problem is how to get *both* kinds of generality at the same time. The question in American education that we have not yet answered is: How can we devise studies that everybody can master but which nevertheless will apply to a wide variety of situations by virtue of their theoretical power?

The classical realist would attack the problem by asking, "What powers are common to all mankind?" And he would answer that the powers to acquire knowledge, to use it, and to enjoy it are the powers that every human being has as part of his human nature. Therefore, he would say, general education should try to form the habits of acquiring, using, and enjoying knowledge. And for the whole school population, with all of their individual differences, we should try to form these habits to the limit of each person's capacity. This is the classical realist's solution of the problem of general education in our time.

Answers to Objections

Is not classical realism excessively wedded to the past? Does not this preoccupation with the dead and gone make learning irrelevant if not downright boring?

I would not say that it is wedded to the past, if this means that classical realism has promised to love, honor, and obey, in good times or bad, for better or for worse. It *is* a kind of love affair, but it involves a selective loyalty. We use the past, but we use it as a source of models of excellence rather than revering it for its own sake. Therefore, it is really not a marriage as such and probably never will be. It is a one-way appreciation of the past.

As regards its alleged irrelevance I have never known anything excellent to be irrelevant. On the contrary, I would think that a thing is classical because it is forever relevant. A model of excellence is always relevant, in our time and in any other time. As for its being boring to pupils, I would expect that it is the dull, the mediocre, the average, that would be boring, rather than these models of excellence.

Has not science shown us that human nature is flexible and changeable, not fixed and universal? How, then, can the realist maintain that there are certain truths and principles which hold for all times and places?

First I would like to know what science has shown this and when science has demonstrated, for example, that being free, or actualizing our own potentialities, or having an integrated life were bad, and for what people and in what culture and at what time in history they were bad. I would also like to know what science has satisfactorily demonstrated that the opposite of these were good—restriction, slavery, not actualizing our potentialities, having a disintegrated personality. In that sense, no one has shown that human nature is not a constant. What I think has happened is this. Studies have shown (I use "studies" rather than "science") that in different cultures different ways of achieving freedom and self-actualization and integration have developed. These are cultural differences, but to recognize them is a far cry from saying that human nature is always changing. It is something like saying that because every grain of sand is a little different from every other there is no uniformity of atomic structure.

Is not education in the pattern of classical realism quite inadequate as preparation for a world which is changing as rapidly as ours?

I have often wondered what kind of education would be adequate in a world that is changing so rapidly. Only one thing could possibly suffice, the search for a pattern that is not changing at all. If the world is changing, all schools are bound to be out-of-date; they can never keep up with the changes no matter how hard they try. The task of education becomes completely hopeless if there is no fixed pattern of the human good, of the good life—a pattern which stays and abides amid these changes and which makes sense out of them. Without such a pattern, I do not know what there is left for formal education to do.

Is not the classical realist's approach to education too intellectual? Do not most people live on a plane which calls for education at a different level and of a different kind?

For the classical realist, education *is* intellectual. It tends to emphasize symbols, language, and theory. I would argue that if this is not what the school does then there is not much excuse for having a complicated system of formal schooling, since the other outcomes we might mention can probably be achieved just as well outside of school.

As to whether this approach is not too intellectual for the kind of life most people live, I dare say it is. We live in an unusual time. Never at any time in the history of mankind have people needed so little brains and so little effort to live *pretty* well. In a way it is the glory of American civilization that people with very little effort and very little knowledge can do extraordinarily well for themselves in the material phase of life. But oddly enough, never before have we needed so much knowledge and so much effort to live *really* well. Or to put it another way, I suppose that never in the history of mankind have so many people lived so well on the brains of so few. Thus we are required to make a decision. At what level shall our people live? Pretty well? If pretty well, I would agree with the objectors that we are probably giving people too much schooling already. If, on the other hand, we want them to live really well, we are not giving them nearly enough schooling and the schooling we are providing is not intellectual enough.

An Example for Illustration and Comment

(This is a portion of the discussion in a high school physics class.)
TEACHER: Today in physics lab we are going to devote our time to a preliminary study of Sir Isaac Newton's three laws of motion. If you have read your homework carefully you will be able to tell me which law I shall be illustrating as I roll this ball across the table. Mary Ann?
MARY ANN: The law of inertia. This means that when something is moving it does nothing itself to change its motion.
TEACHER: That is half of it. Can you tell me the other half?

MARY ANN: Yes. When something is at rest it remains that way until, something moves it.

TEACHER: Good. This ball will continue to roll until it is stopped by me or by some other force. This brings us to Newton's second law of motion. Arnold, will you state it for us?

ARNOLD: When anything is made to move, its motion is in strict proportion to the force acting on it.

TEACHER: Exactly. You boys on the baseball team will know what I mean when I explain the theory of the fast ball and the slow ball. That brings us to the third law of motion. Mary Ann?

MARY ANN: I don't really understand this one. But it says that the action and reaction are equal and opposite.

TEACHER: Let me illustrate it for you. It has to do with the truth that rest is a balance of forces. For instance, this book as it stands on the table is attracted by the force of gravitation, but the strength of the table resists this force, so the book remains at rest. Arnold?

ARNOLD: May I ask a question?

TEACHER: Yes.

ARNOLD: Well, Sir Isaac Newton lived a long time ago. Why are we studying about him today?

TEACHER: That is a good question, Arnold. In any field of learning, whether it is mathematics, science, or even music, there are certain basic fundamentals and truths. Sir Isaac Newton, though more of a mathematician than an astronomer, discovered the laws that explain why the moon goes around the earth and the planets revolve around the sun. Now, our whole modern machine world also exemplifies the same Newtonian principles. For instance, modern rocketry is an application of Newtonian physics. So Newton is really very modern after all.

In this example we have a teacher trying to induct the class into a field of knowledge, an organized, systematic body of knowledge, physics in this case. They are discussing the laws of Sir Isaac Newton, who illustrates one of the peaks of excellence in the development of physics. This is certainly compatible with the emphasis of classical realism. Notice also the concern for the theoretical, for understanding general laws, which is also characteristic of the classical realist approach.

What the example does not and really could not show, because of its brevity, are the arts of learning: the forming of habits of acquiring, using, and enjoying knowledge through engaging in these acts day after day until the student becomes adept at them. Among these are the arts of reading, of studying, of research, of deliberation, and of discussion. Nor does the example show the arts of imagination being developed. For that we might use a different kind of lesson, such as one in the fine arts, in literature, or even in history.

Concluding Suggestions

I will restrict my closing recommendations to two. First, I recommend the reconstruction of the traditional subject matter curriculum. Some of the more recent studies in the mathematics, physics, and chemistry curricula of the high school have selected and concentrated on the key ideas of their subject. Some call them "big ideas," pervasive ideas like gravitation, or chemical bonds, or the axiomatic basis of mathematics. It has been found that children can learn some of these ideas earlier than we thought they could and that they are easily motivated to learn them. Children who approach these subjects in this way are said to find their study "exciting." If we are to have a program of general education following the regular subject matter pattern, this reconstruction will have to be carried out in all the fields. A great many factual details will have to be dropped out; we cannot cover them all in general education. But what is left must be rigorous and theoretical.

My second recommendation is that we try hard to complete general education by the end of the secondary school. There is no reason why we cannot do it. The average boy or girl can finish it in twelve years. Some may need a year or even two years more. But if we could eliminate from the secondary curriculum the prevocational and vocational specialties and really concentrate on general education, then we might get it done, and get it done well enough so that the colleges will not have to try to do it over again.

CHAPTER 3 · Education for
Life Adjustment

Florence B. Stratemeyer

- Human beings, just like every other form of life, must make a satisfactory adjustment to their natural and social environment if they wish to continue effective living. There is a sense, then, in which life adjustment can be said to be the universal philosophy of education. Education is the means by which older generations pass on to younger ones the accumulated wisdom about how to live successfully. So almost by definition, good educators of every age have been motivated by a life adjustment ideal.

    But life adjustment as an explicit philosophy of education has emerged in the United States only within the past 20 years. In its theoretical base, it stems largely from the philosophy of John Dewey and from progressive educational thinkers like William Heard Kilpatrick, who most effectively and fully developed the educational consequences of Dewey's thought. Life adjustment education also represents a response to the needs for universal education in an industrial democracy, in contrast with the need for educating a small elite group, as in most earlier societies.—EDITOR.

- *"Modern living is more complicated with each new day. Our democratic and social institutions are dependent, as never before, upon a greater diffusion of knowledge and understanding. To provide an education that will function effectively in the lives of all children and youth, the school must relate what has meaning for the learner and the basic values of society. This requires a curriculum in which the problems and interests of everyday living which have meaning for children and youth are the starting point. From these immediate concerns, new insights are developed and dealt with in such a way as to provide sound bases for future action. This happens when present concerns or situations of everyday living are seen in the light of continuing life situations—keeping well, understanding self and others, making a living, adjusting to the natural environment, dealing with social and political structures and forces, developing a sustaining philosophy or set of values. These are the situations that recur in the life of every individual in many different ways as he grows from infancy to maturity."* [3]

STATEMENT OF THE VIEWPOINT BY FLORENCE B. STRATEMEYER

Life adjustment education has come to have many meanings, some educationally sound, some unsound. As I conceive it, life adjustment education has two essential elements: first, to help children and youth develop the skills, the knowledge, and the attitudes basic to dealing intelligently with immediate situations of everyday living; and second, at the same time to help them understand the persistent aspects of those situations which recur throughout our lives.

For example, everyone over and over again faces the problem of "What shall I eat? What is a sound diet for me?" The immediate situation of the very young child may be, "Do I have to eat my spinach?" or "Why can't I have my candy just before dinner?" For the youngster entering adolescence, the immediate situations change. Perhaps they are, "What causes the blemishes on my skin?" or "What will happen to my figure if I eat thus and so?" Some of us who are older no longer face these situations, but we deal with the same persistent life situation, "What shall I eat?" Our immediate concerns tend to focus on such questions as "Will my digestive powers allow this type of food?" or "What about fatigue?" or "What are my needs in the light of the last cholesterol count?"

As another illustration, a situation that recurs over and over is that of selecting leaders. It is a situation faced by elementary school children when they select the captain of their team, the individual to represent them in an assembly program, or the editor of the school paper. High school youths deal with the same persistent problem when they, too, select the editor of the school paper or the president of the student council, or when they study and vicariously share in the local or national election. Adults deal with the same problem in relation to their voting responsibilities.

The decision to build the educational program to help children and youth develop the knowledge, skills, and attitudes necessary to cope with the immediate situations of everyday living, and at the same time see the persistent or recurring aspects of these immediate concerns, rests, on the one hand, on the character and values of our society and, on the other hand, on what is known about the learning process. We start with the immediate situations faced by the child for two reasons. First, they provide the material that has meaning for him, that is closely related to his purposes, and we all know that individuals respond and learn in the light of their own purposes. This, of course, does not mean that the educational program is limited by the level of the child's present purposing—quite the contrary. The teacher has the important role of extending the learner's purposes and of developing new purposes through the environment provided by the school.

The second reason for starting with the immediate goes back to the point about meaningful experiences and is found in our belief in the worth of the individual and in the part that he should have in local and national affairs. This requires *individuals who act on thought*— individuals who accept responsibility and whose action is based on reason. The person who acts on thought can act only on the basis of what the situation means for him.

Consider now the emphasis placed on helping the learner see the persistent aspects of immediate situations. Studies of transfer show that the individual will be able to use more of what he has learned in new and different situations if the knowledges and skills are learned in situations similar to those in which they are likely to be used. The changing nature of our society, particularly technological advances, make it unusually difficult to act in accordance with this concept of learning, because in a rapidly changing society the individual must use his knowledge and skills in widely varied and changing situations, for which the school cannot possibly prepare him. Today's children must be prepared as never before to meet and deal with the unknown, with problems and situations now unknown to all of us. Therefore, we must look to the constants in life, the persistent situations which man has faced, faces now, and will face over the years. These are the elements that are and will be similar as children and youth face changing situations—situations which are now unknown to you and me. This, very briefly, is what life adjustment education means to me.

Let me summarize the position in these points. I see it first as a program which opens the doors to fields of knowledge so as to help children and youth select and organize facts, concepts, and ideas, and develop skills in ways in which they will be used in life today and in the future. Second, it helps learners to relate facts within a subject and among fields of knowledge as needed in dealing with problems or situations. Third, it leads to action based on understanding. Fourth, the program is one which contributes to learning that will continue at a high level of competence, since recurring situations call for the repeated use of that learning. Fifth, it is possible for the school to vary its role to meet the needs and interests of its particular children, both by helping them cope with the situations they are meeting in their community, and by adjusting the amount and kind of help given each person in relation to what other educational agencies in the community, such as the home, are providing. Sixth and last, it is a program that minimizes the artificial barriers between life in school and out of school.

Answers to Objections

Is not life adjustment education at most suitable only for elementary and perhaps secondary education, but nothing beyond?

Indeed, I would not agree with that. It seems to me that the life adjustment concept applies equally well to elementary, to secondary, and even to college education. My reason, quite obviously, is that the way in which people learn is the same at all levels. Adults employ the same principles in learning as do children and youth. Furthermore, we want learners at all levels to act on thought.

Is it not true that life adjustment education is rather trivial and superficial? Does it really provide depth of understanding?

First I would suggest that life adjustment is a concept in which the learner's level of maturity determines the depth to which he will go in any area of study at any particular time. We do not exhaust the meaning of a subject the first time we teach it. The safeguard to depth lies in using the persistent life situation concept, which insures that the student will meet this situation over and over again. Also, as we help him work with it at more mature levels, greater depth accrues.

Second, we must not forget that when youngsters grapple with one of these problems, they dig deeply. Furthermore, when they turn to a field of knowledge in search of information, they do more than get information; they also look at the method of the field, which gives them real power and depth of understanding.

Does the life adjustment approach to education really concern itself with the *intellectual* growth of boys and girls?

It surely does. Dealing with the practical, as we would naturally be doing from this point of view, calls for judgment. It calls for action based on thought, as I have already emphasized, and this requires cultivation of the intellect far beyond gathering knowledge for knowledge's sake. It emphasizes high levels of knowledge attainment, to be sure, but it is also concerned with developing interest in learning, with methods of inquiry, with ways of relating facts, and with the ability to use ideas in practical settings.

Does not life adjustment education assume that children are all about the same and make no special provision for the education of gifted children?

Two of the fundamental persistent life situations that I think best illustrate ways of providing for the education of young people with special abilities and interests—the future statesmen, the future composers, perhaps even the future philosophers—are using leisure time wisely and earning a living. Dealing with these problems provides opportunities for individuals to develop both personal interests and vocational competences in keeping with their special talents. I would be the first to say that children who have special interests and aptitudes in music or art, the budding scientists and machinists, individuals with an interest in writing or with a concern for international diplomacy, must be given opportunity to develop their abilities and have extensive experiences in these fields.

The flexibility inherent in the point of view under discussion provides for the gifted child's satisfaction of his greater demands, be they for depth, for creative expression, for abstract reasoning, or whatever. This is more than providing for the normal differences among individuals. If we are going to provide for these specialized talents, we probably need to do some different things than we are now doing in our schools. For example, I would like to see special laboratories in various subjects, in which students with special talents might spend part of their time working with teachers who have special competence. Furthermore, as an individual youngster is ready to make a systematic study of a subject, he ought to have that opportunity, but only when he also knows how to use what he learns functionally in everyday living.

Does not life adjustment education teach youngsters to adjust to society as it is? What about the necessity of educating to change society?

Adjusting to life situations, that is, meeting and dealing with these situations of everyday living and seeing the persistent elements in them, should never be interpreted to mean accepting society as it is. We must be careful to distinguish between adjustment as a psychological term and its use in the sociological sense. By adjustment we do not mean conformity, and we do not mean mediocrity. In fact, there is a fallacy implied in the question, because it suggests that situations are met and dealt with in isolation. This, of course, is not true. Experience is developmental, and when the individual deals with the situation, and sees a cause-effect relationship, at once there is a new cause, and a chain reaction is established. Each experience affects every other experience, and no experience can ever be exactly repeated. There is always movement either forward or backward. Any sound educational program aims clearly at forward movement toward more complete realization of the goals it has set for itself, and the improvement of society as well as of individuals is surely implicit in these goals.

An Example for Illustration and Comment

(A teacher describes an incident in her class):
My name is Mary Patterson, and this is my fourth grade class. Today we had a fine learning session which was not in the lesson plan. It grew out of a question while I was taking attendance this morning. Let me tell you about it. . . .
It began when I found that Joan was absent again.
"Does anyone know why Joan is not here?" I asked.
A hand shot up.
"She has the measles." This was her best friend, Patty.
Another hand in the air. This time it was Timmy, to volunteer the fact that he had already had the measles.
"How many other children have had the measles?" I asked, and about a dozen raised their hands.
Then Richard asked his question. "Could we catch the measles from Joan?" he wanted to know. "She was in school Friday."
Before I could answer, some of the children were nodding their heads in assent while others were shaking them in denial.
"Let's find out," I suggested. "How much do we really know about measles?"
That's how the discussion began. When I saw that none of the children were very sure of their facts, I dispatched a committee to the school nurse and another to the school library. A third group volunteered to draft

a get-well card for Joan. I decided to add "incubation" and "communic-able" to the week's spelling list.

The committee members reported to the class and a good discussion followed.

It is hard to tell much from so brief an episode. But I am interested in this teacher's ability to be flexible, and to recognize a concern that was apparently very real to the children. I hope, however, that she did not start working on the problem without exploring whether it was an area of study that the children really needed; that this was a real opportunity for advancing the children's learning and not just a matter of capitalizing on a momentarily aroused interest. I hope that as she worked with them further she helped them deal with such persistent life situations as local measures for protection against disease, the various ways in which disease is controlled, and personal health routines.

One of the things I miss in the example is evidence that the teacher is helping the children to deal with such equally important persistent life situations as how to attack a problem and how to share in planning the way in which they are going to work. In this particular episode, the teacher apparently made the decision that there would be three committees and where the committees would go. This is something the children should have had a share in doing. Even if they were skilled in such processes, it would have been well to see if they could apply their skills in a new and different setting.

Concluding Suggestions

First, I think it is necessary for professional educators and for laymen and parents to clarify what is really meant by life adjustment education, that is, to outline the essentials underlying the point of view, and check them against what is known about the way individuals learn.

Second, individual teachers, groups of teachers, parents, and other laymen who are interested in gaining greater understanding of what this point of view means might well take the step of cooperatively identifying the everyday situations that their children face, and at the same time of identifying the persistent problems that are part of those situations.

Third, teachers and others could begin by testing this approach in one area of the school program, setting aside a block of time to work on problems and situations with which the teachers feel most competent to deal. Teachers need to learn to work this way. It requires a degree of flexibility and none of us should be discouraged if at first things do not go just the way we want them to. Perhaps one of the greatest pitfalls is the tendency to retain old and familiar ways of behaving that do not contribute to this approach.

Fourth, through conferences, PTA meetings, and workshops, we should provide opportunities for teachers, parents, and other laymen to work together and understand what each is doing in educating children and youth. Only then can home, school, and community complement each other. From the life adjustment point of view this is especially critical, because the same persistent life situations are met in the home, in the school, and in the community, and if we do not work together we can do great harm to children.

Finally, we need to develop a quite different kind of preservice teacher education, in which the prospective teachers can gain experience in this way of teaching. But this is a big subject in itself!

CHAPTER 4 · Education for
Intellectual Discipline

Arthur Bestor

• Education for intellectual discipline emphasizes the unique function of reason in human life. Down the centuries there has stretched a great line of rationalistic thinkers, including the Stoics and Neoplatonists, the Schoolmen of the Middle Ages, the scholars of the Renaissance and of the Enlightenment, and, in modern times particularly, the mathematical and theoretical scientists. Following their lead, intellectualists in education have emphasized the noble traditions in letters and science and have urged the subordination of all other teaching and learning to the nurture of the mind.

Champions of this position, who are often found among academic scholars and teachers in colleges and universities as well as in the more traditional and formal schools, in recent years have been vigorous critics of the vocational, recreational, social, and psychological concerns of modern public education.—EDITOR.

• *"The primary job of the school is the efficient transmission and continual reappraisal of what we call tradition. Tradition is the mechanism by which all past men teach all future men. . . .*

Basic education concerns itself with those matters which, once learned, enable the student to learn all the other matters, whether trivial or complex, that cannot properly be the subjects of elementary and secondary schooling. In other words, both logic and experience suggest that certain subjects have generative power and others do not have generative power. When we have learned to tie a four-in-hand, the subject is exhausted. It is self-terminating. Our knowledge is of no value for the acquisition of further knowledge. But once we have learned to read we can decipher instructions for the tieing of a four-in-hand. . . .

It has, up to our time, been the general experience of men that certain subjects and not others possess this generative power. Among these subjects are those that deal with language, whether or not one's own; forms, figures and numbers; the laws of nature; the past; and the shape and behavior of our common home, the earth. Apparently these master or generative subjects endow one with the ability to learn the minor or self-terminating subjects. They also endow one, of course, with the ability to learn the higher, more complex developments of the master subjects themselves." [4]

STATEMENT OF THE VIEWPOINT BY ARTHUR BESTOR

Education for intellectual discipline means education designed to produce a disciplined mind. What is a *disciplined* mind? Some people are fantastically confused about the matter, asking, in effect, "How often should you spank a child in order to give him intellectual discipline?" Discipline is not a matter of punishment, it is a matter of effective training. A disciplined sailor is not one who has spent half his time in the brig. He is a man who has learned in advance how to respond with effective action to every kind of emergency, whether produced by wind or sea or rock or enemy fire.

The man with a disciplined mind is a man equipped to deal, by intellectual means, with the problems that are bound to confront him in the complex, rapidly changing world of today. Because he has learned to *analyze* a situation, instead of being taught merely to *adjust* to it, he can go to work at once, efficiently and without panic, when he finds himself in a new and unexpected situation. He can summon up resources from the past. He can put to use intellectual skills he has already mastered. Thanks to intellectual discipline, he will *use* his head, not *lose* it, in an emergency.

This kind of discipline is essential to modern civilization. Although we know that science and mathematics are vital to the society in which we live, we often think of them as being essential only to scientists and those who are working with the newest machines. In point of fact, science and mathematics are necessary today for every citizen. Whether atomic energy is to be used for war or peace will be determined by citizens who know enough about the scientific principles involved to make intelligent decisions. Besides the sciences there are the humanities—history, language, and literature. Disciplined knowledge of all these fields is essential to effective participation in present-day society and hence must be diffused to all the children of all the people.

How do we get intellectual discipline in a society? We know that to preserve the public health we need a medical profession and hospitals. Similarly, for the sake of intellectual discipline, we have schools, colleges, and universities. Schools, colleges, and universities exist for the purpose of furnishing intellectual discipline. Athough they may, it is true, furnish other things on the side—just as a hospital furnishes food as well as medical care to its patients—the central purpose of schools, colleges, and universities, is unmistakably intellectual discipline. As Mr. Fadiman said very well in the quotation heading this chapter, many things can be taught that contribute nothing to making the mind a more capable instrument. There is all the difference in the world between learning a manual skill and acquiring the powers of mind that constitute intellectual discipline. Mathematics involves intellectual discipline, but learning how to bake a cake—although it is a very useful skill—does not prepare the mind to deal with the multitude of new problems that a person must continually face.

If we look for what Mr. Fadiman calls the "generative" subjects, we come down to five general categories. These do not include everything that is important, but at least they form a nucleus for any sound curriculum.

First, an educated man or woman must be able to use his mother tongue effectively. He must be able to read and write; so he must study English. Second, in a world where all nations are thrown so closely together, every person must know something about a foreign language and have some ability to speak it if need be. Indeed, most scholars believe—and I believe—that no one can ever know his own language well unless he knows another language. Third, the study of history is essential for anyone who hopes to function effectively in the continually changing modern world, for such study yields knowledge of the past, which is simply the accumulated experience of the human race, and it prepares one to face the fact of change. Fourth, no one could possibly deny that today the sciences are more basic to life, and hence to learning, than ever before. Fifth, underlying the sciences, and valuable as an intellectual discipline in its own right, is mathematics. Thus, English, foreign languages, history, sciences, and mathematics constitute the core of any sound program of intellectual discipline. The charge that these basic intellectual disciplines are outmoded is refuted by even the briefest glance at the facts of modern life.

Moreover, all these subjects should be learned cumulatively. In mathematics, for example, we cannot simply look up the calculus in the encyclopedia and go to work with it. Long building is required to create the necessary intellectual command. In any sound educational system we must strive for cumulative learning, beginning early with the basic concepts and moving steadily forward to increasing levels of abstraction, until finally the highest intellectual powers are developed.

Finally, in a democratic society, we must see to it that every one of our future citizens is carried as far along this main highway of intellectual discipline as his abilities enable him to go.

Answers to Objections

Is not emotional growth part of education, too? How does education as intellectual discipline help a person develop emotional maturity?

Intellectual discipline and emotional discipline go hand in hand. We must learn to control our emotional life for higher purposes. When we say, as did the Greeks, that man is a rational animal, we do not mean that he is always and under all circumstances rational. The ideal is to make his conduct rational as far as possible. Indeed, modern psychology is in part an attempt to understand even the irrational in rational terms for the sake of getting the irrational under control. It is through the disciplined use of intellectual powers that we gain a greater insight into our emotions and hence a greater ability to use them constructively.

Since education as intellectual discipline draws chiefly on the supposedly unchanging truths from the past, how can it be useful to young people in these rapidly changing times?

There is a large element in knowledge which *is* unchanging. We must teach that two and two are four today just as they were in Plato's day and just as they will be in the twenty-fifth century. A great deal of what we do depends on the unchanging truths of mathematics. When, however, I discuss the fundamental subjects, I prefer to justify them in terms not of their unchanging character but of their obvious relevance to today. It is conceivable that a century or two hence certain sciences will have become relatively more important than they are today, and yet the scientific method, the truths of mathematics, and the basic natural laws on which all science rests will be unchanging. Even though the history written two centuries hence will deal with things we have yet to experience, it is the whole sweep of history that is important for man to understand, and nine-tenths of that will always be relatively unchanging.

Is not the intellectual discipline approach to education too bookish? Should not education include more emphasis on direct experience?

Reading books is, of course, one important kind of experience. Also, what I described as the basic subjects include ones such as the sciences, which, if they are to be learned effectively, must be learned through laboratory work as well as through books. Nonetheless, my view does rest on the assumption that books are among the most important of the tools that men have for living their lives effectively, for disciplining their emotions as well as their minds, and for developing the abstract powers that can then be applied to practical purposes.

Does not this position suffer from irrelevance to today's problems? What possible relevance, for example, could Plato's thought have for the young people of today?

It is relevant because it deepens our understanding of our own problems. We do not intend to reconstruct Plato's Republic, but his analysis of the essence of justice and of what happens to a government when justice ceases to prevail is certainly as relevant to the United States of America, which Plato never conceived of (he did not even know of the existence of the continent on which we live), as are many discussions of politics in much more recent times. Plato's thought is basically relevant to the higher purposes of man. If we were not a democratic society, if our children were not to grow up to be citizens with a voice in the future welfare of their country, we could risk depriving some of our children of an education in the liberal arts and sciences. But if we expect them all to be responsible citizens, they must all have the kind of mind that has been produced by disciplined study in the past. We cannot create a workable democracy by rejecting intellectual discipline on the ground that it is an aristocratic virtue. Instead we must make it a democratic virtue by giving it to all men.

I see intellectual discipline as the kind of education which can most effectively help us achieve that excellence we need as a nation, if we are to survive. This excellence is not that of the chrome plating on the front of an automobile. It is the excellence that must be built into our institutions. What counts is ability to maintain the fundamentals, not the superficialities, of our way of life. Intellectual discipline is essential if we are to prove to wise men and women everywhere that the principles for which we stand are valid.

Examples for Illustration and Comment

(The scene is from a twelfth grade class in American history.)
TEACHER: Today, boys and girls, as we begin our study of the Civil War, or the War between the States, as it is called in many places, I want to emphasize one thing. It is important that we learn the facts! Even in a controversial topic such as the Civil War, there are certain facts that are the same no matter what our emotional views may be. We will begin to study these facts today. . . .

We all know that a Civil War is a war between two sections or areas of the same country. In the American Civil War these two sections were the Northern States and the Southern States that had seceded from the Union.

First, we must know which states seceded. Charles, can you name the first state to leave the Union?
CHARLES: South Carolina, on December 20, 1860.
TEACHER: Right. Now, can anyone name the next five states? . . . No one? Well, write these down: Alabama, Florida, Georgia, Louisiana, Mississippi. These states formed the provisional government of the Confederate States of America on February 8, 1861. Jefferson Davis was chosen president the next day, February 9. Yes, Charles?
CHARLES: But there were more than six states in the Confederacy. When did they come in?
TEACHER: An excellent question. During the month it took to form and adopt a permanent constitution, Texas, Arkansas, North Carolina, Tennessee and Virginia also seceded. The western counties of Virginia refused to secede, so the state of West Virginia came into being. What happened as new states came into being is a lesson in itself, and we will talk about that tomorrow.

Note that the teacher asked the students to acquire a certain amount of basic information. So far so good. But the example does not give us enough of a view to indicate whether instruction stopped with mere facts. If so, it led nowhere. I hope the teacher went on to show her students how to think—how to use information as the basis for careful reasoning about cause and effect, about the relation of historical events to their geographical setting, about the fundamental issues in the great conflict. Only if history is taught as a way of thinking about men and events—thinking grounded in knowledge— can it achieve its purposes, one of which is to enable students to face the problems of their own day with a long historical perspective.

(The leader of a Great Books discussion group sums up:)
"Tonight we have been talking about Plato's *Republic*. Written by one

of the immortal thinkers of ancient Greece, the *Republic* outlines an ideal commonwealth in terms still applicable today.

We have seen that Plato exercised great influence on all subsequent human life and behavior. His ethical vision, his practical wisdom, and above all his methods of inquiry have guided thinking men throughout the generations.

It was Plato who expressed the fact that man's superiority over animals stems from his ability to form ideas, and it was Plato who pointed out that one of the most important systems of ideas man has invented is contained in mathematics, through which he can order his knowledge of the universe. Today our scientists are just beginning to show the lengths and depths to which Plato's type of thinking may yet carry us."

The discussion itself would have been more useful than the instructor's summing up, for telling us whether this was a valuable introduction to the great thought of the past. Learning comes not from talking *about* a book, but from reading it and discussing the ideas contained in it. Once these ideas are understood, provided the book is really a great one, they will have immense applicability to our present problems.

Concluding Suggestions

My practical recommendations are these. First, every high school should offer at all times a full roster of the courses that are absolutely essential—English, mathematics, science, history, and foreign languages.

Second, in our comprehensive public high schools, to which many of our ablest young people are going, courses must be available to them at a level advanced enough to challenge them—a level as high as in any selective school, private or public, here or abroad.

Third, it is not enough merely to offer subjects. We must make sure that the work done in each course is of a high degree of seriousness. The sciences must not be taught from books alone but also in laboratories. Good writing must be taught by requiring the student to write and write and write, and by making sure that his themes are graded and discussed by the teacher.

Fourth, we must be sure that the ablest students are pushed along toward higher levels of understanding at the maximum speed they can maintain. At the same time, we must have streams in which slower learners are being taught the basic disciplines instead of being shunted off into speciously "practical" courses.

Fifth and finally, and this is the heart of the matter, there must be public support for serious intellectual training in our schools. The public must insist that the schools engage in serious intellectual work and not waste time on things that are of trivial significance.

CHAPTER 5 · Education for
Psychological
Maturity
Arthur T. Jersild

• Many observers of present day life have pointed out the frightening difference between our remarkable understanding and control of the physical world and our meager understanding and control of ourselves. These observers go even further in believing that education, which is mainly concerned with intellectual knowledge and technical skills, really serves only to aggravate our present human predicament. Those who believe in education for psychological maturity draw heavily on the insights of modern depth psychology—stemming from Freud, Jung, Adler, Sullivan and others—about how the human mind develops and why people behave as they do. They also have recognized anew, and now they have clinical support for their position, the wisdom about human nature that is contained in some of the great religious, philosophical, literary and artistic traditions of both Eastern and Western culture. Thus, Plato and Jesus, Buddha and Shakespeare, St. Augustine and Kierkegaard, are in fundamental agreement with modern clinical psychologists in asserting the primary importance of a person's inner life and in the ideal of education as the care of the soul.— EDITOR.

• *"Education should help children and adults to know themselves and to develop healthy attitudes of self-acceptance. The crucial test in the search for meaning in education is the personal implication of what we learn and teach. We must make an effort to conduct education in depth, to move towards something that is personally significant beyond the façade of facts, subject matter, logic, and reason behind which human motives and a person's real struggles and strivings are often concealed. To encourage the process of self discovery we must raise the question of personal significance in connection with everything we seek to learn and everything that is taught from the nursery school to post-graduate years. What does it mean? What difference does it make? What is there in the lessons we teach, the exercises we assign, the books we read, the experiences we enter into, and in all of our undertakings, that can help us to find ourselves, and through us help others in their search?"*[5]

STATEMENT OF THE VIEWPOINT BY ARTHUR T. JERSILD

The philosophy of education I advocate was voiced by Socrates when he said, "Know thyself." I believe that while teaching the basic subjects we should give more attention to the personal meaning of what we teach and the personal concerns of the students whom we teach. I also think we should recognize the simple fact that each human being has emotions, and that to live effectively he must learn to acquire a certain amount of harmony between his ability to think and his ability to feel.

My view further takes account of what I regard as certain dangers and hardships within our culture. Our emphasis on impersonal subject matter has far outweighed the effort we have made to promote growth in emotional maturity. Large numbers of children and adolescents move toward adulthood with unresolved emotional problems, worries, anxieties, fears, grievances, and feelings of guilt and self-reproach. In some people these problems explode in delinquency, crime, and other forms of acute distress. But these problems also place a burden on large numbers of people who outwardly seem to be well adjusted. In most of our education I think we have ignored this burden. We teach students about almost everything except about themselves. Deeply ingrained in our culture is a policy of evading the inner life while we turn our minds to the learning of impersonal things.

I think this policy of avoiding the inner life is a stereotype, a vestige from primitive times, and does not truly reflect the potentialities of the human mind. I believe that human beings from an early age have more capacity for acquiring knowledge of themselves than we have assumed in our theories. People have more capacity for acquiring thoughtful and realistic attitudes of self-acceptance than we have encouraged in our educational program.

So I propose that efforts to promote self-understanding should be incorporated into the total educational program, from the nursery school on through the ensuing years. This is basically an educational problem, because the ideas and attitudes that constitute a person's evaluation of himself are not thrust upon him ready-made; they come into being through a process of learning. And the encouragement of good learning is the essence of education.

Now what do these premises imply? They imply that as members of the community we should insist that the school should give more attention to mental health. They also imply that in the teacher-training program we should give more attention to the emotional dimension of human existence—the affection and compassion, the striving and hope, the currents of anger, guilt, fear, anxiety, and grievance that course through the lives of all human beings.

They imply further, I believe, that we should as far as possible incorporate into the educational program the insights that can be gained from psychology, psychotherapy, and psychoanalysis and from the humane branches of existential philosophy which emphasize the struggle an individual faces in finding and being himself. This does not mean that we are assigning a new task to students or to teachers. They already are engaged in this task and have been since they were small children. Each in his own way must seek to live with his own emotions. What I am proposing, as I see it, is simply that we try more frankly, openly, and honestly, to face issues that everyone faces, and always has faced but usually without help, within the secret and lonely reaches of his private life.

How do young people respond to this approach? I have worked on that subject for some years now, and the answer is that some don't respond, but that many others, among the young as well as the older students, are eager to cope with their personal problems if given the chance to do so with a person whom they trust.

How do teachers respond? In one of my studies I found that over 90 per cent of about one thousand teachers endorsed the idea that education for self-understanding should be an important part of the school's program, and about half of these people said that in order to carry out this program they would need help in dealing with the personal and emotional concerns of their work as teachers. This does not mean that teachers now have to become professional psychotherapists. Teachers can help to heal the wounds of life even if they do not pretend to be full-fledged therapists. I have also found that those who have gone the farthest in their search for self-understanding are those most likely to recognize the dangers, the possibilities, and the limitations in this field as far as classroom work is concerned.

The view I am advocating is designed mainly to promote the learn-

er's personal well-being, but it also has important scholarly implications. On the one hand, as all teachers know, unresolved emotional
problems are a barrier to learning. On the other hand, anything a
student gains in understanding himself adds to his wisdom as a
scholar. The student who has gained a deeper knowledge of the forces
that flow through his own private life will have a deeper understanding of poetry and drama, history, philosophy, biology, economics,
aesthetics, and all of the scholarly disciplines.

Answers to Objections

Isn't it likely that such a psychological approach to education would
lead to entirely too much self-preoccupation on the part of youngsters?

I feel that in trying to help young people to understand themselves
we are not creating preoccupations; we are helping them to get out of
the vicious circle of preoccupations that already exist. There are
studies that show that the typical elementary school child, for example,
has many worries and fears that oftentimes neither his teacher nor his
parents know about. A child who is worried is already a preoccupied
child. I do not think we create fear by trying to help a youngster to
cope with fear. There are also studies that show that high school and
college students have serious personal concerns. There is the public
scholar who goes through the academic motions, there is the hidden
scholar concerned with problems within his own private life. We do
not create problems in these people by helping them to bring their
problems out into the open.

This approach presupposes great competence on the part of teachers.
How can we expect to prepare teachers to deal effectively with the
emotional life of children?

If we are to put into effect the idea that I have expressed previously,
we shall have to overcome our compulsion to try to do it overnight. I
would further point out that teachers are already deeply involved with
the psychological welfare of their students. They tamper with the
emotional lives of their students when they ignore them, when they
pronounce failure on them, when they fail to recognize their symptoms
of anger, fear, and other forms of distress. Hence, the alternative to
trying to help youngsters to understand themselves would be to proceed unknowingly and yet still deal with them from a psychological

point of view. What I am advocating is that what now is oftentimes done somewhat unknowingly should be done more knowingly, and with compassion.

Should not the responsibility for the emotional development of children be carried by the home rather than by the school, which has other primary functions?

The home, of course, is the primary source for the creation of the child's attitudes toward life. But there are many forces in a child's life outside the home that have a very important effect on his attitudes and on his views of himself. In one of my studies, I found that the children had more worries connected with school than worries connected with life outside of school. In another study it appeared that with respect to experiences at school the young people expressed more self-reproach than self-regard and confidence in their own worth. So I would say that while the home is very important, the school also has a tremendous role in molding the lives and guiding the mental health of students.

If it is true, as many critics assert, that our schools are falling behind in the teaching of fundamentals, how can we justify bringing into the school these additional and significant, but tremendously difficult, emotional problems for the teachers to cope with?

I don't know how far behind we are falling in dealing with the fundamentals. I think achievement tests show that we are keeping up with the pace pretty well as compared with twenty or fifty years ago. But, without quibbling over terms, I would also ask what are the fundamentals? And what could be more fundamental than to help a growing person to make full use of his powers and to deal effectively with the problems that arise in his personal life? I think that the most fundamental preparation for tomorrow is to learn to live adequately today.

Would not this kind of education be very expensive? How can we do it unless we have very small classes?

Of course, if the teacher has a smaller class he can give more attention to individual students. But in the last three years or so I have been working with about one hundred teachers who have tried to work along the lines that I have suggested, and all of them have been working in classrooms of regular size. I do not think we have to delay the proposals I have made until all the physical and financial conditions are perfect. We can do something with them right now.

An Example for Illustration and Comment

(A teacher speaks.) "This is my fifth grade at Anderson School. It is a large class, but a good one. The first week of school I was just busy sorting the children out, so to speak. Now I'm getting to know them—the slow ones, the bright ones, the dreamers. They're taking the weekly arithmetic quiz now so I can catch my breath a little." (A boy throws a spitball.) "There, did you see that? That's Tommy's work. Sometimes I think he's deliberately trying to get into trouble. He doesn't even seem to mind staying after school. I wonder what can be troubling him."

(Later) "I decided to make Tommy Jones my special project tonight, and I'm glad I did. The more I examine his past records, his aptitude tests, his previous report cards, and teachers' comments, the more puzzled I am. Tommy's attitudes and behavior since the beginning of this school year are definitely contrary to the excellence of his former work. Something is keeping him from doing his best. I had the school nurse check Tommy's vision; sometimes faulty vision shows up at this age and brings behavior problems until it is detected and remedied. But Tommy's vision was 20/20 and his hearing was perfect too."

(She visits Tommy's house) "A visit to his home seemed to be my next move. I think I knew the answer to Tommy's problem before I entered the house. For nearly 12 years Tommy had been an only child, and now there was a baby in the picture to threaten his security, to compete for his parents' love and affection. A few moments' conversation with Mrs. Jones confirmed my theory. It was the old story; the new baby demanded so much time and attention that Tommy was being ignored, unintentionally of course."

(She concludes) "Not quite understanding what was disturbing him, Tommy had tried to meet his needs by creating disturbances in class, by being boisterous, and by being rude to his friends. Well, he didn't revert back to the old Tommy overnight, but the change did come. Through careful cooperation of his parents, Tommy became the all-important big brother with nothing at all to fear from the infant in the crib. Within a few weeks he was once more the alert, well-balanced student. His work improved and so did he."

This example does illustrate the way in which an emotional problem can block a child's learning. In this case the trouble came in an arithmetic class. It also shows the way in which an emotional difficulty may lead to behavior that gets a child into more difficulty, sometimes producing retaliation from teachers or from others. In this particular instance, the teacher seemed to feel a little threatened by the fact that the student was having trouble and was being obstreperous. But instead of striking back at him she stopped to inquire what might be underneath his behavior, and as it happened the problem worked out pretty well. In this case, the source of the problem was located in the home, in the relationship between the boy and his parents and the new little baby.

Many problems do have their origin in the home. I do believe, however, that sometimes school people try to evade problems that are localized within the school by seeking causes outside the school. I am not now denying that these causes outside the school do exist, but I mention this because in the literature during the past ten or twenty years there has been a good deal of criticism of parents, a tendency to make them the authors of all the world's woes. Of course parents have their frailties and difficulties—they are human beings—but I do think it is important for school people to recognize that the child's life is determined by many forces both inside and outside the school. So it is important, as far as possible, to have compassion not only for the child, but also for his parents.

Concluding Suggestions

As members of the community we should be more alert to the possibilities of promoting mental health through the school and should support efforts within the school to achieve that purpose, even though they are sometimes fumbling.

We should give much more attention to the emotional dimensions of our lives and should encourage teachers, parents, and others to share their feelings with one another. This takes courage, because the barriers against it are very strong, but some people are able to acquire that courage and get a great deal of benefit from the sharing.

Furthermore, teachers should be encouraged to examine their own attitudes through what they perceive in others and the feelings they have toward others, because what we see in others is oftentimes a projection of something in ourselves.

Next, I suggest that teachers who desire to get psychological help should be encouraged to do so and should not be frowned on or looked on as queer people, as is now sometimes the situation when persons seek help and have the courage to admit openly that they can be aided by others in their search for a deeper understanding of the issues of their lives.

Finally, in the education of teachers, we must provide more opportunity for sharing experiences within the group. We need to help teachers to deal with the underlying feeling-tones as distinguished from the superstructure of logic that so often is the only thing touched on in teachers' meetings and in committee meetings. I think the possibility of going beneath the surface is far richer and offers far greater returns than we have so far been able to realize in our work with one another.

CHAPTER 6 · Education for
Moral Character

Ernest M. Ligon

• All human societies have principles or codes of moral conduct. All have ideas of right and wrong. Whenever realization of these ethical standards is taken as the major objective of education, we have a philosophy of education for moral character.

This philosophy has a long and distinguished history. Aristotle's *Ethics* is one notable expression of it from ancient times. In Far Eastern civilization, Buddhist and Confucian teachers emphasized the development of ethical character. Obedience to the moral law has been a dominant motif in the Judaic-Christian tradition for more than 2500 years. Among modern philosophers, the principal exponent of the moral outlook is Immanuel Kant.

Moral concern is now both more urgent and more perplexing than ever before. Vast cultural changes have forced revisions in many customs and have brought about a re-examination of moral standards. At the same time, the complexities of modern life and the new powers made available through science have made ethical controls of greater importance than ever before. Modern moral philosophies of education are a response to the need for character development adequate to the demands of contemporary life and responsive to the insights of contemporary knowledge.—EDITOR.

• *"All education is moral, for the end of all teaching is to complete the moral growth of the child, and to impart to him the moral ideals of the race. No knowledge is merely for its own sake, but all must in some way affect conduct. Children act as they have been taught, or as society has let them teach themselves. Honesty, truthfulness, industry, and the other essential virtues of the moral life can be taught. Moreover, the ethical end is not a far-off culmination of one's education, but an idea that is to be realized in every step of the educational process. The child is to grow continuously in the moral as in the intellectual life, and these two aspects of life are inseparable. Every study is to contribute directly to the growth of the moral self."* [6]

STATEMENT OF THE VIEWPOINT BY ERNEST M. LIGON

Most of our national leaders agree that it is far more important to have strong moral character in our citizens than to have good rockets, yet as a nation we have done astonishingly little with character education. Research in this field has demonstrated fully that most traditional approaches to character education will not suffice. For example, great strength of character does not result from negative ethics—from telling people what not to do. Not very long ago, I was talking to a group of twelve- to fourteen-year-old boys and asked them first what it was wrong to do. Since they had been majoring in that for some time, they knew many answers. They told me it is wrong to steal, wrong to lie, wrong to hit young children, and so on. Then I asked them what it is right to do, and they had no idea whatsoever. Finally one of them did say, "It's right not to steal and not to lie," but when I rejected this answer and said, "No, I want you to tell me not what it is right *not* to do but what it is *right to* do," they did not have a single suggestion.

The key to strong character is to define to youth what it is right to do and to challenge them to build moral and spiritual strength with a positive approach. However, knowing what is right to do is no simple task. Ours is a very complex world. Once in a while a parent will say, "My child knows the difference between right and wrong." I am always envious, because every day I face a dozen problems in which I am not at all sure of the difference between right and wrong. Our world is so exceedingly complex that character education today consists, in part at least, in discovering what are the right and wrong things to do.

It takes skill as well as will to do right. Today's older generation may have meant well, but did not have the skill to carry out their good intentions. So character education must be concerned with teaching young people *how* to do the right thing, even after they know what it is. For example, I have not deliberately set out to make anybody angry in forty years, but I have done it many times, always unintentionally, because I have lacked skill in right human relations. Hence, we must try to give young people the skills as well as the will for moral conduct. I would define character as having the courage, the will, and the skill to live up to the convictions that one believes to be central in the very universe itself.

Are there practical methods of communicating moral knowledge and teaching moral character to the young? If we want to develop a dominating purpose in a nursery child, we do not simply say to him, "I hope you will grow up to have dominating purpose." We teach him that it is more fun to build blocks up than to kick blocks down. Or again, how shall we help youth to go about the task of channeling their emotions? There used to be much talk about how to control temper by counting to ten, and so on, but nobody ever got very far that way. Then we came to realize that emotional energy is an inherited characteristic, just as physical energy or intelligence is, and that what matters is how it is invested. We can invest our emotional energy in the negative emotions—fear, anger, hate, and suspicion— or we can invest them in the positive emotions—faith, enthusiasm, love, and high vision.

In bringing about this positive channeling, we must take account of the particular child, the person as an individual. If, in a group of acquaintances, each person were asked to submit an anonymous description of some of his recent temper experiences, and then if the members of the group were asked to decide who had done which, they could easily be identified. Thus, to find out how to channel our emotional energy, it is necessary to consider carefully the effect of individual differences. Character education consists in finding out what each child is like and dealing with him accordingly.

Another crucial problem is that of communication. We do not preach to youngsters, but we do help them to know and do right. In this process we are often trying to teach them to learn something that we do not know. If we had known it, we would have done a better job in our own generation. We had plenty of good will, but not enough good skill. So we attempt to communicate to young people the best that we have done, at the same time saying to them, "We hope that you can do a far better job." Thus, we work *with* them.

Finally, it is important to consider the factor of social influence. We may do good, and still carry no social influence at all. Let me illustrate by referring to a group of some two hundred high school boys and girls from all over the country, who are concerned with this problem of social influence. They say that only about five per cent of teenagers are really bad, and that another five per cent are so highly skilled socially and have such wonderful personalities that they can successfully oppose the group when the group tells them to do something they do not believe is right. However, the other ninety per cent, who are not bad, still do not have the skill and ability and hence are afraid to stand against the crowd for fear of losing out socially. These two hundred young people for the past two years have been sending in their reports of experiences in which they have had to go against the crowd. These reports relate what happened and then give an evaluation of these experiences. Some students report the social influence they carry in holding to their convictions. On the other hand, some tell of what they have suffered, because of standing up for what they believed to be right. The young people involved in this project plan to convene and attempt to apply scientific techniques to discover some of the skills needed to stand up for what is believed to be right. These high school students are confident that they will discover some new things that can be put in a book to be made available to teen-agers all over the country, which will give them the skills by which to stand by their convictions. It is just as important to develop the skills to do right as the will to do it.

Answers to Objections

Since moral judgments are so different from one person to another, how can we educate for moral values?

Although there are many differences in our moral convictions, there are also many similarities. Just as the principles of physics and chemistry are in the very nature of the universe, so are the moral principles. Congress could not set out to pass a law that hate will henceforth be better than love. Love is better than hate, just in the nature of the case. Legislators could not make fear better than courage. Courage just is better than fear; that is the way the universe was made. There are many such universal principles.

Therefore, even if we do differ somewhat in our basic convictions, character education is still possible. You will recall that my definition of character was having the courage, the will, and the skill to carry out our convictions, whatever they are. It is not so much the convictions that make character, as are the determination and the ability to carry out what one honestly believes.

Can goodness really be taught?

Of course it can. Every once in a while somebody makes the statement that character is caught, not taught. I am never quite sure what this means. If it means that in everyday life we catch our character from whomever we meet, we are doomed never to improve, because everyone meets all kinds of people. Trying to keep a child from catching the wrong kind of character is like trying to keep him from catching the measles. On the other hand, if we mean by "caught," deliberately exposing him to certain kinds of influence, hoping that he will be inspired by the kind of people we want him to be inspired by, that is character education. Character education is not a matter of saying, "Now, boys and girls, be good." It takes place through discussing with them how they may practice what they already believe. We begin by persuading young people that we are trying to help them with something they believe in and then go on to work out the skill to accomplish it.

Are not moral values a proper concern for the home and the church but not for the school, which cannot properly handle such debatable issues?

That question interests me, because some of my colleagues in religion are continually telling me that character education does not belong in the church school, but that it ought to be done in the home and the school. Now it is suggested that it ought not be done in the school, but in the church and home. Someone will point out next how hard it is to get anything done about character in the home. So it looks as though everybody is trying to put it off on somebody else! But to answer the question directly, I think everybody who has any influence whatsoever on the child has an obligation for developing moral character. The school has the child for more of his waking hours during his growing-up period than does any other institution, even the home, and therefore the school ought to do something about character education. I believe, moreover, that character built on a religious faith is likely to be stronger and finer than character that lacks such a foundation.

In our pluralistic society, is it not improper to introduce religiously-oriented values into the public schools?

I seriously doubt that what I call the religious values of moral character would in any way violate our principle of separating church and state. For example, objectives which I would call specifically religious in their nature are these: a dominating purpose in the service of mankind, a love of right and truth, faith in the friendliness of the universe, sensitivity to the needs of others, the will to make conflict creative instead of destructive, and the determination to carry out convictions, whatever the cost. I believe that most people would approve of these values for their children, regardless of their religious creed or affiliation.

How, specifically, does a properly educated person deal with a moral problem differently from one without benefit of good character education?

Again, it is a matter of skill. For example, when a person with appropriate skills faces a situation that would ordinarily make him angry, or inspire fear, he regards it as an opportunity to discover how to make a positive emotional response. As a result of many years of research, I am convinced that we can channel virtually all of our emotional energy into the positive emotions. One practical procedure for teaching channeling skills is to have children describe the situations in which they are tempted to be angry or afraid, and then to consider in each case how they can make reactions which are positive instead of negative. It is very interesting to watch them do this—even at the nursery and kindergarten age levels—and to see them challenged by the process.

Some young people, and older people too, who were quite sure they could not control temper have found methods of doing it. A young engineer came to me not long ago, and said, "For years people have been telling me to control my temper, and I couldn't do it; but this channeling idea, I can take hold of. I know what to do about that."

An Example for Illustration and Comment

(Here are some excerpts from an actual discussion at a youth conference devoted to character research and development):
LEADER: Well, what about those learning goals? What have you come up with? John, what steps can you take?
JOHN: I found that there were four people with whom I don't get along at all. I can't see why, either. My goal is to see if I can understand why I or the other person get angry when we do. If I could get a whole list of these, maybe I could do something about them.
LEADER: Mary, how about you?

MARY: I suddenly realized that when I get angry with another girl, for instance, I start a bad rumor about her. I don't want to be a gossip, so I guess the best thing to do is to start a good rumor about her.
LEADER: Bill?
BILL: Well, I find it very hard in athletics when an opponent plays dirty against me, not to try and get back at him. I wonder if next time when he does something good a few plays later, if I shouldn't compliment him on it?
JANE: I have a sister who gives me lots of good practice. She sure hits me enough. If I can just not sock her back, I'll have to improve a whole lot.
FRED: I know what it means to get mad. I do it too fast. But when I get over it, I can hunt for something my brother needs, and try to see that he gets it.
ALICE: That's like my goal. I find I get mad at people. Why, after we're both over it, we're too stubborn to take the first step. We refuse to speak to each other for days, sometimes weeks. From now on, I'm going to take the first step, whether I'm right or not. I always think I am.
ROY: There's a boy in our class whom nobody likes, because he won't let you like him. He's soured on life. I'm going to break through his bitterness and make a friend of him if it's the last thing I do.
SUE: I get mad when my mother asks me to do the dishes more often than I think I ought to—which is never—but hereafter, I'll do it, and even if I get mad at the time, I'll find something else to do around the house, too.
JIM: Both my parents are cheek-turners. I'll go to them first for advice, and ask them to teach me the skills, to help me make it work.

Notice three chief characteristics of that discussion. In the first place, the leader was not telling the young people what to do. The young people were trying to discover skills for dong what they thought was right. I refer to this as the method of *creativity*. At such a conference, the young people are reminded that their elders do not know all the answers to many of the problems of today, for if they did, our present difficulties with race conflict, crime, and so on would not exist. It is up to the young people to discover their own answers. Thus, they are asked to set as learning goals the finding of solutions to problems which are real in their own lives.

Second, the problem must be *difficult*. Too frequently in moral training young people are asked to do small things. Dealing with anger constructively is a difficult problem. Young people must be challenged to use their best. At one youth conference I warned them that our schedule was quite impossible to complete, but teen-agers do not know the meaning of the word "impossible" and so, much to the astonishment of all of us, they carried it out, and did a far better job than I had supposed they could do. For example, before the conference I had outlined some conclusions they might be expected to reach. When the conference was about two-thirds over, I instructed them to forget my conclusions, because it was obvious to me that they were reaching results far more significant than the ones I had planned in advance.

The third characteristic to be noted is that the matter must be *significant*. Young people want to make a difference in the world in which they live. The members of that youth congress were working at making a socially more harmonious world. At one youth conference, the young people were reminded that for every one of them there were 150,000 teen-agers like him in this country, and that what each of them could do, each of the 150,000 could do. What each of them could not do, the 150,000 could not do. That impressed them deeply and all during the conference, every time they thought about letting down, they would comment on the 150,000 teen-agers who were depending on them. They were sure that they were going to make a difference in the world as a result of their experience and their discoveries. I have already mentioned, for example, the hope of discovering a series of principles that can be put into the hands of all teen-agers that will make them able to live by their convictions, regardless of social pressures. The young people who have been participating in that project for more than two years now are convinced that they are going to help change the whole world. I believe they will!

Concluding Suggestions

Any teacher or parent trying to give character education to children of any age level, even as far down as the kindergarten, can use these three principles I have mentioned. In the first place, the experience must be made *creative* so that the young person as well as the teacher finds answers, with the teacher admitting to begin with that he does not know all of them. It also has to be an experience that is meaningful to the young person himself, one that relates to his own real problems. The child needs help in learning something that even his parents and teachers do not know.

Second, the student must be given something exceedingly *difficult* to do, that uses all his powers. It must not be so hard that it frustrates him, nor should it be so simple that he feels it is not worth doing.

Finally, the tasks assigned must have social *significance,* so that young people realize that what they do is not just something for themselves, but something that will be of value to the society and to the country in which they live.

I think these principles can be applied by any teacher or parent to make character education much more effective than it has usually been.

CHAPTER 7 · A Protestant View of Education

Merrimon Cuninggim

- A part of the genius of Protestant Christianity has been its encouragement of a wide range of viewpoints on most subjects. In this, education has been no exception. Thus there are many points of view on education that can be called Protestant. At the same time there is a central Christian tradition beginning with Jesus and the Apostles, and reaffirmed by Luther, Calvin and the other Reformers that provides a basis for convictions about teaching and learning.

  In Europe, the Protestant Reformation exerted great influence in support of popular education. This grew naturally out of the Protestant insistence on individual responsibility before God and the importance of every believer's being able to read and understand the Bible. In America, Protestant Churches have taken a leading part in the advancement of education at all levels. They early founded colleges for the education of clergymen, and later for instruction in all of the branches of higher learning. They have also, for the most part, been vigorous promotors of free, universal public education, in spite of the problems that are raised by seeking to relate a religious faith to the public schools in a pluralistic society.—EDITOR.

- *"Education divorced from religion is doomed to spiritual sterility; religion divorced from education is doomed to superstition. A dogmatic religious faith and a dogmatic secular philosophy of education are bound to be mortal enemies, but religion and education, in proportion as both are honest, informed, and humble—that is, truly liberal—are natural allies. In other words, if religion is man's search for, and response to, ultimate meaning, and if education is man's total preparation for a meaningful life, it follows that only religion can give ultimate meaning and depth to man's aspirations, and that only education can make these aspirations intelligent, informed, and creatively effective. So defined, religion and education are both absolutely essential to man's perennial quest for responsible freedom and enlightened dedication."* [7]

STATEMENT OF THE VIEWPOINT BY MERRIMON CUNINGGIM

The first thing to say about a Protestant view of education is that there is no such thing. Protestant views of education there are in abundance but there is no one view that alone can be said to be authentic. This might be taken by some people to be a kind of weakness in Protestantism. Folks might say, "Protestants don't know where they stand because they can't get together," or, "They can't get together and thus they don't know where they stand." Actually this would be a serious misconception. Rather, it ought to read, "Protestants don't agree on any one thing, education or anything else, because they *do* know where they stand."

This takes us to the heart of what Protestantism is all about. The two words, *Protestant Reformation,* provide some insight into the character of the great movement by that name which began in the sixteenth century. Its early leaders were engaged in *protest* against what they thought were abuses in the church of that day, and they sought *reform* of those abuses so that a better church could come into being. Now anyone engaged in protest or reform must be able to speak his own mind, and thus there was built into the Protestant position the right of private judgment. Diversity is part of the Protestant tradition and part of the Protestant belief. I can't speak on this subject for all Protestants, nor can anyone else, and the fact that I can't is itself a Protestant principle.

There are some other principles, too, in a Protestant view of education, on which there has been considerable Protestant consensus through the years. Some of the old watchwords remind us of them. For example, "the priesthood of all believers," which means that each man has direct access to God and must serve as his neighbor's priest, or "the authority of the Bible," from which follows the need to read and understand the Bible.

These great beliefs, some of which Protestants share with other Christians and with Jews, serve to make up a kind of testimony on the problem of education or anything else. So, if someone would ask what this means for education, I think the answer would be quite clear. Protestants, first of all, are committed to education by virtue of their being Protestants. In order to read the Bible, to know the nature of their calling in the world, to understand better their relationship with men and with God, the Protestant must search diligently, must develop his own capacities as far as possible, must seek to replace ignorance with knowledge, and immaturity with maturity. Thus as a fundamental principle Protestants must believe in education.

Once this is said, there are two special things to be said about a Protestant philosophy of education. First, Protestants believe that schools must be good schools and colleges must be good colleges. Now it could easily be said, "Of course, everyone believes that. What is distinctive about that?" I do not claim that there is anything distinctive, but I do insist that it is part of the Protestant heritage to drive toward excellence in education. Time and again, it is true, Protestants themselves have not been fully loyal to their heritage. Many of the great universities of this country, independent and tax-supported, are perhaps truer to the Protestant tradition in this regard than are some of the denominational colleges that seek to put limits on learning and to fetter the free mind. Be that as it may, the Protestant tradition believes in excellence in education and derives this from its understanding of the ways of God and man.

The second special principle is considerably more controversial. For the Protestant, in education, as in every other area of life, God must be recognized as the sovereign of life. Thus, according to a Protestant view of education, some appropriate way must be found of teaching in the schools that man does not live by bread alone, that God is, and that God is sovereign. Some people take the position that neutrality on this matter is desirable. The difficulty with this is that neutrality is not possible. No matter how desirable one or another person of whatever religious heritage, or of none, might feel it to be, it simply cannot be. Our schools and colleges are not neutral on many of the crucial issues of life—on freedom *vs.* slavery, for example, or on knowledge *vs.* ignorance, or on character *vs.* the lack of it. And because educators make it clear that they believe in freedom and knowledge and character, sooner or later they must give those beliefs some kind of ultimate rootage, some kind of cosmic support. If they do not have the conviction that these beliefs are somehow in the essence of things, if they think that all this is simply a relative matter, they will ultimalely have no convictions at all.

The Protestant calls to mind that these values and others in which school men believe must be rooted in a conception of the universe in which God is the ruler. It should be emphasized that this point of view applies to all kinds of colleges and all kinds of schools, not just to parochial and church-related schools. For from the Protestant point of view there is no proper separation of the spheres of life into secular and sacred. All of life is one, and all is subject to God's mercy and judgment. Thus, religion must come into the school program in some proper way—precisely how is a difficult question, which I can't try to settle now. But religion must be united with education, for only as they are made partners have we any hope to see through to a better day.

Answers to Objections

How can religion be introduced into a public school system in a pluralistic society such as ours, where people of many faiths, or none, must be equally served?

This is certainly one of the most difficult questions to be faced. Our pluralistic society does require a nonsectarian approach to the problem. Perhaps we may get some leadings as to how this may be done by considering the relation of religion to government—surely a controversial matter, yet one where we have discovered ways of recognizing our basic dependence on God. "In God we trust," we say. Our stamps and our coins remind us of that, but often our diplomas don't.

Still, I ought to say, lest someone believe that what is desirable in schools is Bible reading and the mention of God every time the child turns around, that many of the efforts now made to introduce God into the educational picture, are (at least to my way of thinking) unfortunate and unwise. We are not called on to bring religion into the schools in any situation in which it does not properly belong. We should not be sectarian any more than we should be secular. Only when religious subject matter properly inheres in the subject under treatment, ought it to be brought in. Only when the religious stance is appropriate to the concern under question ought it to be taken. And there do come times in the life of every school when such mention and such notice are appropriate, and at these times a secular philosophy of education is seriously deficient.

Does not the introduction of religion into the public schools in any form violate the Constitutional principle of separation of church and state?

I think not. Perhaps we do not fully understand all that is allowed or proscribed by our so-called principle of the separation of church and state. It seems quite clear to me from a study of its historical development that this principle was never meant to eliminate all relationship of religion with government or mention of religion by government, or vice versa. In its origin, this principle called for the disestablishment of a special church that had a special relationship with the state. When this disestablishment took place, first in Virginia, and then in the other colonies that had various degrees of religious establishment in colonial times, this move was called "separation." It was brought about by dissenting groups who were seeking their own freedom or full equality for their religious groups in the eyes of the law. That is to say, it was brought about by religious interests; it was not a blow aimed at religion, but it was, as some scholars have called it, a staff to support religion and religious equality in our country.

We therefore have in this nation a double principle of relationship between religion and government. The particular phrase we use often calls to mind only one of the two aspects of this relationship. We do have a separation of church and state as organic entities—an organic disconnection, if you will. The second aspect of the relationship is one of sympathetic association, which was present when the separation principle was enunciated. This sympathetic association exists and has existed through the years in all of the countless ways by which our government recognizes and encourages religion on a nonsectarian basis.

Constitutional principles do prevent sectarian practices, but it is part of our American system that government may and ought to note that religious faith is at the heart of our democratic way of life, and that God is supreme.

Assuming that religion were to be introduced in some way into the school as you suggest, how could teachers possibly be prepared to deal competently with so difficult and controversial a subject?

This question suggests one of the great weaknesses in our present practice. Certainly most of even our best teachers are simply not competent to speak about theology or about religion. Many of them are hardly competent even to point out the relationship of religious thought to their own particular subjects and disciplines. This is one

of the areas in which a great deal of work needs to be done. However, it is too much to ask that all teachers be fully educated theologi-
cally. It *is* right to ask that they be informed laymen in respect to
their own faith, whatever it is, and that, without bootlegging religion,
they take proper note of the religious perspective in the treatment of
their particular subject matter.

An Example for Illustration and Comment

(A Protestant Christian minister speaks as follows in closing a sermon
for Christian Education Sunday.)

"In summary, the goals of Christian education are these: First, to lead
the student into a personal relationship with God. The primary purpose
of good Christian education is to see that the individual student becomes
a closer ally of God. Second, to give to the pupil an understanding and
appreciation of the life and teachings of Jesus Christ, and to lead that student into being one of his loyal followers—not merely into an academic
understanding of Jesus Christ and his teachings, but into becoming an
actual follower. Third, to ecourage the student's enthusiastic participation
in the building of a Christian community in a Christian world. But only
by beginning with activity in the local community can one prepare for
larger influence in the making of a better world. Thus a fourth goal is to
develop both the ability and desire to participate actively in the life and
work of the student's own Christian church. One who is educated from a
Christian point of view should be interested not only in the distant scene
but also in influencing lives close at hand. Human beings are like fissionable
material; they influence one another in chain reactions. Fifth, one of the
goals of Christian education is to train the student in the discipline of piety
and the mechanics of competence. It has truly been said that, "Piety without competence is as bad as competence without piety." The total personality is the goal of one who is being educated according to the teachings of
Jesus Christ. Sixth, and finally, Christian education should give the student
the positive working knowledge of the matrix of human wisdom, namely
the Holy Bible. For this is the source from which comes human wisdom in
its highest form. Amen."

On the whole, this is a good statement of the goals of Christian
education. Nevertheless, for the purposes of our discussion, I'm in-
clined to think that it departs from the topic with which we have been
concerned here. This minister has spoken of a philosophy of Christian
education, whereas our theme is a view, a Protestant view, of education in general. This example permits me to emphasize the fact that
the analysis I have presented is not meant to apply specifically to

Christian education, but to education in general, and what it means from the Christian standpoint. Most if not all of the things that this minister said in his sermon, would be inappropriate for the public school, for it is necessary that the public school be nonsectarian. The last point he made, about the desirability of knowing the Bible as one of the great monuments of our Western culture, could be translated, I think, and ought to apply to any kind of educational system, public or private. But his other points are mainly concerned with specific Christian training, which the church, not the public school, must give attention to. My own point, which this example doesn't touch, has been that education in general—what we often call (but shouldn't call) "secular" education—must give recognition to the Source of knowledge, and the Author of truth, because it aims to be good education, not because it aims to be Christian or "religious" in any way.

Concluding Suggestions

Practical measures to apply this philosophy are not easy to suggest, but I will make two or three points. First, I want to emphasize that this whole question needs to be opened for discussion among school men at the elementary, secondary, and college levels, and among teachers of all subjects, all across the country. It's a strange thing that we are afraid of this topic. We tiptoe whenever anyone suggests that God ought to be brought into the public school. I do myself. I'm nervous about some of the ways in which some people interpret this suggestion. I don't want prayers lugged into a school system where they don't belong, nor Bible readings inserted that offend one or another segment of our population and that are essentially irrelevant to the task of the school. Thus I say our first task is to discuss this subject and see what is possible, what does make sense in our school system from top to bottom as we know it.

Beyond this, we must develop a willingness for careful experimentation, for trying out some ways of making clear the relationship between education and religion. There are a host of such experiments going on now in our country. I know of one in a teacher's college in which the faculty have been brought together to discuss these questions from the standpoint of the religious perspectives of their own particular disciplines. I know of another in a state university in which the teaching of religion as a subject is being approached. As a matter of fact, many state universities are providing for such a program now. There are fruitful experiments going on all across the land and we need to expand these.

What ought to be said in conclusion, however, is simply this: the Protestant view of education of which I speak, does not ask that any one thing be done. Rather it asks that a certain attitude be felt, namely, that religion and education, both rightly conceived, are partners and belong together. We shall have this puzzling question of *how* they are to be related with us for a long time to come. *That* they belong together, however, is the contention of a Protestant view of education.

CHAPTER 8 · A Roman Catholic
View of Education

Robert J. Henle

- Roman Catholicism is one of the great universal religions of mankind. It is world-wide in scope, and possesses a history of nearly two thousand years, stemming back to Jesus and the Apostles. It is the religion of an organized church with a centralized hierarchical system, and with a well-developed body of beliefs and practices.

  Education has always been of great importance to this church, because of its concern for the propagation of the faith and for the nurture of Christian personality. Fundamental Roman Catholic beliefs about human nature and destiny, about reality and knowledge, and about moral law and social institutions have significant consequences for methods and goals of teaching and learning.

  Philosophically, Roman Catholic teaching tends toward classical realism. While this is supremely exemplified in St. Thomas Aquinas, who in turn drew heavily on Aristotle, some Roman Catholic thinkers emphasize the Augustinian and Platonic form of realism.—EDITOR.

- *"The true Christian, product of Christian education, is the supernatural man who thinks, judges and acts constantly and consistently in accordance with right reason illumined by the supernatural light of the example and teaching of Christ. The proper and immediate end of Christian education is to cooperate with Divine grace in forming the true and perfect Christian, that is, to form Christ Himself in those regenerated by Baptism. For the true Christian must live a supernatural life in Christ, and display it in all his actions.*

  For precisely this reason, Christian education takes in the whole aggregate of human life, physical and spiritual, intellectual and moral, individual, domestic and social, not with a view of reducing it in any way, but in order to elevate, regulate it and perfect it, in accordance with the example and teaching of Christ." [8]

STATEMENT OF THE VIEWPOINT BY ROBERT J. HENLE

Let me begin by asking why there is a Roman Catholic kind of education and by answering that it is because there are people in the world who believe certain things. They believe that God exists, that He is a Triune God, that He sent His only Son, Jesus Christ, into the world to save and to teach mankind, and that as God's messenger Jesus Christ taught certain facts which are essential to the living of a good life and to the securing of happiness.

They believe that He not only taught these facts, but that He also held up certain moral ideals, gave us principles of conduct, and demonstrated for us a way of living that would lead man to happiness both in this life and in the life hereafter. These people believe further that in order to bring these benefits to every human being Christ founded an institution, a Church that was to last to the end of time, not merely as an organization, but as a means of carrying His authority and His message to all times, all places, and all peoples, and that He would be with this organization, guaranteeing through its teaching the purity of its original doctrine.

If this is the framework within which a Catholic thinks of life, then obviously Catholic education will have to fit into it. Thus, we want to start the child from the very beginning living this life, learning the creed of Christ, learning the ideals and the code of Christ, learning to worship, and learning to use the sacraments. The child is seen by the Catholic to be not just a bundle of electrons and atoms, as a materialist might consider him, nor just an animal—not even a superfine kind of animal, the high point of evolution. To the Catholic, the child, from the moment of conception, is a person who does indeed have a body and lives in the material world, but who also has a spiritual soul and for this reason is fundamentally and radically different from the material universe and anything in it. This person becomes of value, someone of quasi-infinite worth, loved by God.

Moreover, although the child has intellect and therefore freedom—the power to be a responsible individual—God so loves him that He has planned that the child should have a new level of life. The child should have not only the life of the body and of the mind, not only the ordinary life of a human being, but a life of divine love which in a true sense is a sharing in the divine life of God Himself. Thus we try to move the child from his undeveloped, dependent state by the development of the body and of the mind and of the will and by the continual development of the divine life which he has from the moment of baptism. This divine life, which shows itself in action as a life of love, we would consider as the perfection toward which we are moving the child. It is not only a perfection of what might be called the natural potentialities of the child, but finally a perfection of supernatural love.

We regard education from the very beginning as resting upon these assumptions and being governed by these ultimate perspectives. Hence it is impossible for Catholics to think of having a school system or any form of education that would not at all times be permeated with these beliefs. And so, in a Catholic school, the reality and presence of God, the reality of Jesus Christ, the guidance, the teaching, and the influence of the Church, and the ideals of the Christian life, are constantly presupposed. Within this integral framework all of the physical and intellectual disciplines have their appropriate place. Because all of education is seen within the context of God's creative love and as leading ultimately to the salvation of the child in a loving union with God and with all men, it is possible to be open to every kind of good development in human culture. This is evident in the school curriculum. Although we do indeed teach the creed and doctrine of Christ, belief in the Trinity, and the meaning of the sacraments, we also teach such subjects as arithmetic, social studies, and history but always with the awareness of God's providence and love.

In Catholic education, all human good can be brought to the children but constantly against this Christian background with this Christian interpretation. For example, in the study of history, although it is a strictly scholarly task to determine the facts of history, the Christian interprets them in the light of his belief in the providence of God. The case is similar with other subjects in the curriculum. Thus, the child is introduced to the whole of culture, but in such way as to bring him ultimately to the full perfection of Christian living, of Christian independence, and finally, in the next life, to the full love of God and union with Him.

Answers to Objections

Is not Roman Catholic education dogmatic, is it not based on the assumption that truth is absolute and is known, and does it not contradict the approved modern point of view that truth is tentative and hypothetical?

First let me say that the view that we really don't know anything, that all our truth is tentative and hypothetical isn't particularly modern. It is older than the Christian position, older than Plato, as a matter of fact.

I take exception to calling this the approved modern point of view. If you leave a few academic philosophers to one side, the average intelligent and educated person takes a view something like this. There are some things which we know for sure. We know, for example, that England is an island and that the moon shines by reflected light. These are facts. They are not tentative. No geography teacher says, "Children, England is an island, but this is quite tentative and hypothetical. It might turn out to be something else." So there is an area in which people agree that there is something known. Next, there is an area of guesses, hypotheses, tentative statements—an area of imperfect knowledge. And finally, there is the vast area in which we don't know anything.

Catholics adopt fundamentally this same commonsense view of knowledge. Where we Catholics differ from non-Catholics is that in the area of what is known, we put in things about religion that the non-Catholic would not include. Obviously, if the non-Catholic thought that among things known was the existence of God, the divinity of Christ, and the institution of the Church by Christ, he would be a Catholic. As for Catholics being dogmatic in general, I would say it is only in these matters of religious belief that we differ. We too have graduate schools in which we try to achieve more knowledge, and we too recognize the tentative and relative character of much knowledge.

Doesn't the authoritarian character of Catholic education encourage young people to believe what they are told rather than discovering truth for themselves?

There is always a possibility of distorting a good position. Here again, we must make a distinction. Catholics want to train youngsters to accept legitimate authority intelligently, not blindly. For example, it would not be intelligent to tell a sick child, "Don't go to the doctor, and don't take his advice; think it out for yourself." We attempt in Catholic education to encourage an intelligent approach to legitimate authority—the authority of courts, of policemen, of parents, of the state, and of the Church. We don't want to make automatons—people who say yes, without thinking. The mature product of Catholic education ought to be a person who accepts legitimate authority intelligently and reasonably, because he understands why it is a legitimate authority.

Does not the Roman Catholic system of parochial school education constitute a divisive force in our society and deprive Catholic youngsters of the opportunity for democratic education with children of other beliefs?

If by divisive it is meant that Catholic parochial schools perpetuate differences in society, it is quite obvious they are divisive, just as are Sunday schools, Jewish day schools, the various churches, and political parties. Such divisiveness is part of our culture. The magnificent thing about American pluralism, as opposed to a monolithic society, is that we encourage people to tolerate their differences, to live with differences. If divisiveness means hostilities and tensions, and this is always an accidental accompaniment of differences, the effort of many of the things Catholics do is to counterbalance and overcome divisiveness. For example, in our schools we teach Christian love and tolerance, on playgrounds and in organizations like the scouts Catholic children intermix with children of other faiths, and Catholics participate equally with other citizens in civic affairs.

As I see it, the alternative to our present system is a pressure toward uniformity that would ultimately and logically lead to a monolithic system of opinion and education. If we want freedom we will have to put up with divisiveness. I have enough confidence in American democracy to think that we can survive our differences.

Assuming that the operation of a separate parochial school system leads Catholics to request the appropriation of public funds to these schools for certain purposes, does this not run counter to the long-established American principle of the separation of church and state?

On this point there are considerable differences of opinion among Catholics—educators, ecclesiastical people, and even parents. My own position is that there ought to be some financial relief to the Catholic parent, although I am not particularly in favor of any grant of public funds directly to religious schools. Since the parent is sending the child to a Catholic school as a matter of conscience, not as a matter of luxury, the provision of free public education from the point of view of the Catholic really has a catch to it, a kind of religious qualification that is counter to the whole direction and spirit of American democracy, which rejects all religious qualifications, negative or positive, for any public benefit.

So I think it is a matter of American principle, rather than of theology or of the wish of the hierarchy, that some way should be found to give the Catholic parent and the Catholic child some share in the common benefits of education. Let me quote a sentence I once wrote which I think states the fundamental principle involved here. "No citizen because of his religion or lack of religion shall be deprived, directly or indirectly, in theory or in practice, of the enjoyment of his rights, privileges, or benefits of citizenship; nor shall the exercise of the duties of citizenship impair his full religious liberty." It seems to me that out of this principle some provision for a fair proportion of aid to the Catholic parent, the Seventh Day Adventist parent, the Lutheran parent, would be in full accord with American principles.

An Example for Illustration and Comment

(A Sister, in garb, is teaching a class in a Roman Catholic school. The room is adorned with a crucifix and pictures of Christ, as well as the usual maps, blackboard, etc.)

SISTER: Children, we have been discussing what will happen to us when we receive Confirmation. We said that Confirmation does these things for us: It makes us stronger Christians, more perfect Christians, and soldiers of Christ. Today we have been discussing this third point—being soldiers of Christ. The first two we said have to do only with ourselves. You children know that Christ did not just say, "Be strong Christians, be perfect Christians," but He gave us, first of all, His example, secondly, His Commandments and directions, and thirdly, some special helps. What did we say those special helps were, Jean?

JEAN: The seven gifts of the Holy Ghost.

SISTER: Good, Jean. The first of these two points have to do only with ourselves, to be strong Christians, perfect Christians. Today we talked about that third point: a soldier of Christ. The first quality of a soldier must always be what?

SAM: Courage.

SISTER: Yes, now let's look at that last point. A soldier of Christ is responsible for others. Let's take that idea and apply it to our social studies. Look at the map for a moment. We have been studying the Eastern States, and we have noticed how these people depend on each other and need each other. All year in our various units we have discovered how interdependent the sections of the United States are. Now children, can you see what the attitude of a Catholic should be toward these interdependent people? Interdependence is not just being a good American. Realizing our interdependence, the need for justice and charity, is part of our Confirmation, part of being a good soldier of Christ. Can you think of some special ways in which these people of the Eastern States depend on each other and depend on other parts of our country?

First, it should be pointed out that this example is taken from a catechism class. It illustrates the teaching of doctrine, which is done formally in classes of this sort. This is not a class in arithmetic or social studies as such, which would probably be taught in a more formal fashion. The presence of various religious symbols in the classroom helps to remind everyone of the religious beliefs which permeate the school. The example also illustrates the effort of the Catholic educator to put Catholic faith and principles into all of the child's obligations, his civic as well as his religious ones.

Finally, I would mention that while the classroom technique suggested in this example is typical of many Catholic schools, as well as of others, further examples would show that a great variety of techniques are used in the Catholic schools.

Concluding Suggestions

I want to conclude with some comments on the bearing of the Roman Catholic position on the problems of the public schools.

It is clear from what I have already said that in the Catholic view, nothing short of a fully Catholic education, in the strict sense of the word, is ideal and nothing short of that will really satisfy the conscience of the Catholic parent and the needs of the Catholic child. So I think the Catholic should gain from this analysis a deeper realization of the connection between Catholic education and the faith itself —those important facts by which the Catholic parent is convinced he can build a life for himself and his child.

But that this is not the whole story should be crystal clear from what

I have said, particularly from the Catholic view that education at all levels is a tremendously important thing for a human being and that to provide education is a universal obligation in any society. This means that although the Catholic wants a Catholic school for his own children, he should also be vitally interested in the education of all other children. The fact that he is a Catholic imposes on him an obligation to be interested in making the public schools of his community the best that can be made for the children who attend them. I might suggest that a parallel attitude on the part of the non-Catholic would also be in the finest traditions of American society and American democracy, namely, an interest in seeing that the Catholic child has the best opportunities for education that can be given him. Both kinds of schools are resources of America. It is within these resources that we want to develop the fine people of the future, while maintaining our freedom and also our spirit of cooperation.

CHAPTER 9 · A Jewish View
of Education

Eugene B. Borowitz

• Judaism is one of the great historic religions of mankind. As a complex system of life and thought, it
embraces a wide variety of viewpoints on many subjects, including education. Therefore, there is no
single Jewish philosophy of education. It is possible,
however, to distinguish certain dominant features of
the Jewish outlook and to suggest certain consequences of it for teaching and learning.

The Jewish community has traditionally given a
high place to the teacher, or rabbi. Scholarship is
honored and study is encouraged as a religious obligation. Since the Bible and the Talmud are regarded
as prime resources for understanding the will of
God, meticulous care is given to their reading and
interpretation. The Hebrew language and traditional practices are also central elements in the
culture thus transmitted. It is significant that in all
western civilization, no people has had as long and
continuous a history of deliberate educational concern as the Jews.—EDITOR.

• *"Learning is acquired by him who knows his place, who is content with
his portion, who makes a hedge about his words, who takes no credit
to himself, who is beloved, who loves God, loves mankind, loves acts
of charity, loves reproof, loves rectitude, keeps far from honors, is not
puffed up with his learning, does not delight in handing down decisions, bears the yoke along with his fellow, judges him with the scales
weighted in his favor, leads him on to the truth, leads him on to peace,
concentrates on his study, is capable of intellectual give and take, is
capable of adding to what he has learned, studies in order to teach,
and studies in order to practice, makes his teacher wiser, is exact in
what he has learned, and quotes his source."* 9

STATEMENT OF THE VIEWPOINT BY EUGENE B. BOROWITZ

The Jewish view of education is based on its view of man. If we start with the Biblical verse which says, "Man is created in the image of God," I think we can understand the Jewish point of view on education. When the Bible said "Man is created in the image of God," it meant that man was not cut off and isolated from the universe, but was part of it. Somehow he could reach out to it and understand it. Man may be limited and small, but he can grow toward God because something in him corresponds to God. This is the first source of the Jewish motive and desire for education.

But there is a second motive as well. Man is not just an animal that can educate itself to be more God-like. Man is a creature of history. Other men—some of them geniuses—have learned about God. Men like Moses and the prophets have written down their experiences in a way that enriches and enlarges ours. Thus, we not only consult our own experience, but we also study the records of men who went before, so that we can better understand ourselves and our relationship to the universe.

It is from this view of man that the Jewish philosophy of education grows. A man needs to study so that he may become himself. Learning is part of his being, part of his very existence. It is a religious duty, a commandment. A man who would fulfill himself continually needs to study, to educate himself.

It is important to recognize that we are talking here about man, not about children. Jewish education is concerned largely with what the adult needs. All through Jewish history we have a record of adults studying and learning. To say this indicates already that Jewish education is meant to proceed all through a person's life. A man grows and changes, his problems grow and change, and perhaps the circumstances in which he finds himself also change. Thus, education must continue on a lifelong basis. Perhaps the most popular picture of a Jew is that of an old man bent over a book.

This view may be somewhat different from the ordinary view of education, but it clearly has implications for the education of children as well. Obviously, if we are to have educated adults—people who will study all their life—we must begin with our children. The Jewish devotion to the education of children is a time-honored tradition. It is a tradition that most people recognize as typical of Jews. Even to this day, when some Jews are not as faithful as they ought to be in following their traditions, devotion to the education of their children still maintains.

But if Jewish education applies to all of a life, whether at one age or another, it is universal to all men as well. A man needs education because he is a man, not because he is old or because he is young, or because of any other circumstances or condition. Therefore, a Jew would not limit education to one group, to priests or to rabbis, to the rich or to the idle. Education should be universal because every man requires it to fulfill himself as a man. It has been only in recent years that Jews have carried out this principle with regard to women as well as men. Today the Jewish view includes the ideal of universal education for both men and women.

At one time, Jewish education was regarded as a personal and a familial responsibility, which every parent carried out for his children. This tradition still persists. Yet, as society became more complex and as the requirements of education grew, as long ago as two thousand years ago, somewhere about the time of Jesus, Jewish education changed from solely a private and familial concern to one in which the community took responsibility. After all, parents are not the only ones who want children to grow up in a certain way; the community also has a stake in their education. So the community provided schools and what were in effect scholarships, it fostered academies for higher learning, and it saw to it that even for the simple man there were special halls where he might go to study. This notion of community responsibility for education has been carried out down to the present day.

Thus, for the Jew a rounded view of education emerges. He sees education as a continuing task, which goes on for a lifetime, which ought to occupy all people, and which begins with the family but stretches out into the community. Perhaps I can summarize it best by citing a statement given us by the Rabbis of the Talmud: "An ignorant man cannot be truly free." Whether we think of our education today as purely religious or in the broader sense of what it does to a man, of how it helps him fulfill his potentialities, it is clear that these statements help us to make religion and education primary goals of our life. If we would know ourselves and understand ourselves, we must study and we must learn. Education is not a luxury; it is the bread of life itself.

Answers to Objections

Is not Jewish education, with its traditionalism, out of keeping with modern needs?

It is a general problem of American life that we are so eager to rush into the future that we pay no attention to the past. Sometimes we are so eager to be "progressive," or "dynamic," or "creative," that we don't know where we have come from nor where we are going. Yes, Jews do think that part of the past is important, but they see the tradition as a base for moving forward, as a direction and a guide to where we ought to be heading. If we look at contemporary Judaism, and at the Judaism of the Classic Periods—the Biblical and Talmudic times—we find that Judaism has changed and developed, and it can do so today. But in caring for the tradition, Jews have a basis on which to change. I think we need such foundations in America today.

Is there not too much emphasis on books and on intellectualism in Jewish education? Does this emphasis not hinder education through direct personal experience?

It is important first to consider the nature of those books. Most of the books out of which the Jews studied were books of law. They were books which had to do with life, with the actual situations in which people found themselves. Jews have no objections to using other instruments of education. It wasn't too long ago that everyone had to study from books because there was nothing else to study from; movies, films, and slides and the kind of life situations that some educators emphasize today are recent innovations. Although I see nothing in the Jewish view of education against using these media, there is still a place for books too, particularly the Great Books, the Classic Books. One of the major indictments of our education today is that so few people have read and mastered the Classic Books. We might have less criticism of education if we had more people who had studied the great Classics. From the Jewish standpoint, studying and understanding the Great Books ought to be an integral part of our education.

Does not the strong and increasing identification of some Jews with the Jewish religious community introduce a divisive influence into the education of young people?

I do not believe that religion really has this effect, even a community religion such as Judaism (a religion which has been practiced in homes and community affairs as much as inside the synagogue). Most divisiveness comes from the attitudes people have toward one another. If one looks at what Protestantism or Catholicism, and certainly Judaism, have to say about getting along with our neighbor, religion becomes a means of sending the individual out to meet his fellow man, to associate with him in a way that benefits them all. It is not the teaching of the Jewish religion or its community activities which brings about divisiveness, but rather the attitudes which people have toward one another for reasons which are irreligious.

It seems to me that what we require in America—and what education requires—are strong religious roots, the kind of loyalty to our own faith which will help us to see our fellow men as creatures of God. Perhaps the best summary of this view is found in the great rule from the book of Leviticus, which was quoted so approvingly by Jesus, namely, "Thou shalt love thy neighbor as thyself." This is what Jewish faith teaches. This is not a divisive influence, but the real basis for democracy.

Jews have generally opposed any introduction of religion into the public schools. Is this not inconsistent with the Jewish concern for religious education?

The essential question here is what keeps religion alive. Would it really be beneficial to religion if the public schools were involved in teaching it? The Jewish people are expert in this question of what keeps a religion alive. We have been a rather small minority for 2000 years, scattered among the peoples of the world, and as a result we know pretty well what can and what cannot keep a religion meaningful and active in the hearts of its people. To introduce religion into the public schools would bring divisiveness into what has been one of the great unifying forces of our democracy. In our public schools a child is not educated as a Jew, or as a Christian, or as an unbeliever, but simply as a child of our country. Religious teaching in the public schools would inevitably divide one group from another, and take what has brought us together and make it an instrument that would divide us one from another.

Besides, has the American principle of the separation of church and state harmed or helped religion? As we see it, religion is stronger and has more active influence in the lives of individuals in American communities than almost anywhere else in the world. Separating church and state has made for a healthy competitive spirit in religion, which has made it grow and prosper. Even though we are a small minority, we Jews are not afraid of the challenge which the American system has given us. We want to emphasize in our homes and our synagogues the things we care about as a faith. But we will pray and hope and work to see to it that the public schools as our major bastion of democracy will always remain free from the teaching of religion—any religion.

An Example for Illustration and Comment

(An observer describes a scene from a Jewish home on Friday evening:)

We are in a Jewish home for Friday night dinner, where guests are always welcome. The Sabbath candles were lighted just before sundown by the mother of the family.

Now the father is concluding the Kiddush ". . . with love and favor Thou has given us Thy holy Sabbath as an inheritance. Blessed art Thou, O Lord, who sanctifiest the Sabbath Day."

No one is in a hurry tonight. In many modern busy homes, this may be the only meal the family eats together all week. This is the time the father traditionally asks what the children have learned in school. He may even quiz them a little. Respect for learning is one of the cornerstones of the Jewish home, and it is enhanced in a family atmosphere such as this one.

Friday night is also the time for recounting the triumphs in the classroom, Joel's "A" in spelling, Ruthie's French paper which drew praise from the teacher. Both are applauded in the family circle.

The children in this family, like many other American Jewish children, attend Hebrew classes after public school hours. Father's questions, at the Friday dinner table, indicate his interest in this area of their education as well.

The young man of the house has a question, something in his Bible study that he didn't quite understand at Hebrew School. He knows that this is the time he can count on his father's unhurried and undivided attention. He knows, too, that father enjoys his role as a sort of supplementary teacher.

Even the mother doesn't mind the interruption of dinner. She is proud that her young son has asked an intelligent question, proud that her husband can answer it. The dinner will wait, for "whoever teaches his son teaches not alone his son but also his son's son, and so on to the end of all generations." So it was written in the Gemara.

I wish every Jewish home were like that! Unfortunately, in our day many families are not doing this sort of thing. However, I think the example does capture the heart and spirit of the Jewish tradition in education. When the little boy brings his book to his father, he knows that his father will be interested and that his mother will be looking on approvingly. This is a father who cares about education, who wants the child to come with his book, who doesn't mind being cast in the role of a teacher, even though he knows that sometimes he won't be able to answer the questions.

Here is a family spirit and an attitude toward education that is quite dear to us and that will make education precious in the life of that child. This home really revolves around education, doesn't it? It is something that is part of the relationship between the father and the mother. Furthermore, there is no confusion between what needs to be done at school and what needs to be done at home. The father cannot teach his child everything, nor can the mother. They want their child to go to school, they want him to have a good school, and they want his teachers to be equipped to teach their child. But the home is the motive force and the source of power. Here is where the educational drive and the goals are given.

A scene like this suggests something which is very precious to Jews, and I think it also hints at ideals and practices which if carried out by families all over America would illuminate the whole of our American education.

Concluding Suggestions

I believe that these Jewish ideals of education are not just for religious people or for Jews alone. I think they contain a message about education that should appeal to every citizen. They suggest something about the way every American adult ought to look at education. Education is part of his life, part of realizing his potential. Self-fulfillment is the great American aim and it is an aim that would strengthen our democracy. When parents, teachers, and every citizen in this country recognize what education can mean to them, education will mean more to our children and will enter into the fabric of our democracy. But more than that, our institutions, our tax problems, our school building difficulties, our standards for teachers and classes would improve if each of us saw education as integral to our way of living. Being a successful American human being entails success in education.

But education need not be limited to the schools alone. Schools can do their part, even in the teaching of some of the goals that religion holds dear, especially in the teaching of moral and ethical values. The relationships between teachers and students, the attitudes of school administrators toward members of their staffs, the ways the public looks at education, all of these can create a moral and even a spiritual atmosphere, in which the child may grow in the way that religious people would want him to. None of this is doctrinal, or is it the teaching of religion in the formal sense, yet it cooperates toward the goals that religious people want. The teaching of religion itself, which would integrate and unite these influences, in our American society would spring from hearth and home.

If anything should stand out of all this, it is a call, indeed a cry, to all Americans to understand what education is and should mean to them. Education is not just a matter of books or of elementary and secondary schools, or even of our great universities and colleges. Education is a matter fundamental to the life of a human being, and insofar as democracy is concerned with human beings, education is essential to the life of our democracy as well. It is to an awareness of this that a Jewish view of education summons us all.

CHAPTER 10 · A Conservative
View of Education
Russell Kirk

• Education is of necessity largely a process of con-
serving. Unlike physical characteristics, culture cannot be inherited; it must be learned. Education is
the passing on from generation to generation of
cultural achievements that make up the fabric of
civilization. Therefore, according to this view, it
is the teacher's duty to preserve and to transmit
faithfully the well-tested ideas and worthy traditions
of the past.

Cultural conservatism is perhaps the oldest of all
philosophies of education. All of the major religions
have been sustained by revered and zealously
guarded traditions. Enduring civil societies throughout history have owed their health and longevity to
respect for the traditions of civility. In western
political life, perhaps the most vigorous expression
of this point of view was given by Edmund Burke,
and its highest practical embodiment has been
achieved in British and American constitutional
government. Conservatives have steadfastly opposed revolutionists, social planners, utopians, Fas-
cists, and Communists, who seek to sweep away the
past and to replace it with some abstract ideal.
—EDITOR.

• *"The very time to avoid chaos in the schools is when something akin
to chaos characterizes the social environment. The very time to emphasize in the schools the values that are relatively certain and stable
is when the social environment is full of uncertainty and when standards are crumbling. Education follows, it does not lead. If education
is to be a stabilizing force it means that the school must discharge
what is in effect a disciplinary function. The materials of instruction,
the methods of teaching, and the life of the school as a social organization must exemplify and idealize consideration, cooperation, cheer-
fulness, fidelity to duty and to trust, courage, and perseverance in the
face of disappointment, aggressive effort toward doing the task that
one's hand finds to do and doing it as well as one can, loyalty to friend
and family and those for whom one is responsible, a sense of fact and
a willingness to face facts, clear and honest thinking. These may not
be eternal values, but one may venture a fairly confident prediction
that they will be just as significant a thousand years from now as
they have ever been in the past."* [10]

STATEMENT OF THE VIEWPOINT BY RUSSELL KIRK

You may have read that short sardonic novel by an eminent conservative, Mr. Evelyn Waugh, *Scott-King's Modern Europe*. Scott-King, a classics master at an English public school, is invited to lecture in a Mediterranean state. Soon involved in sad difficulties, at the end of the summer he finds himself stark naked in a concentration camp in Cyprus. Escaping at length, he returns to his school at the beginning of the Fall term. There the headmaster suggests that he teach some popular subject in addition to the classics— economic history, perhaps; for the classics are not popular. "I'm an old Greats man myself," the headmaster says. "I deplore it as much as you do. But what are we to do? Parents are not interested in producing the 'complete man' any more. They want to qualify their boys for jobs in the modern world. You can hardly blame them, can you?"

"Oh, yes," Scott-King replies. "I can and do." And, deaf to the headmaster's entreaties, he declares, shyly but firmly, "I think it would be very wicked indeed to do anything to fit a boy for the modern world."

Scott-King's point, of course, and that of Mr. Evelyn Waugh, is that if we adjust to error and crime we are, in short, making ourselves privy to error and crime. The purpose of education is not merely adjustment to modern life, but adjustment to something higher, adjustment to *norms*. Norms are what Mr. T. S. Eliot calls the enduring things, the standards in morals, politics, and taste, which have a lasting importance. And that, I think, is what the conservative in education is endeavoring to preserve. This is what I may call *normative* schooling—the teaching of enduring truths. We learn these norms through the traditional disciplines, through great literature, through ancient, modern, and American history, and through the scientific branches of knowledge.

We moderns, the Schoolmen of the fourteenth century used to say, are dwarfs mounted upon the shoulders of giants. Today we seem to ourselves to be superior to the men of ancient times because we see further than they did. But we see further than they did only bcause we are standing upon their shoulders. And if, growing impudent, we give a swift kick to the giants, down we tumble into the ditch, and that is a social and personal catastrophe. The giants represent the wisdom of our ancestors; and we, however high we may stand upon the pyramid of civilization, are by ourselves only intellectual dwarfs. Therefore, if we are to understand the norms which make life worth living, we must turn to inherited wisdom; we must recognize what G. K. Chesterton calls the democracy of the dead. Chesterton meant that we must count the votes, intellectually and morally speaking, of wise men in many centuries—indeed, over three thousand years. They have a right to be counted because it is not simply this generation that is wise. It is the species.

Educational conservatives look to the Schoolmen and to modern writers like Chesterton for guidance, and particularly in modern times to such wise men as Edmund Burke, Samuel Taylor Coleridge, and John Henry Newman in England, and Irving Babbit and Paul Elmer More in America, all exemplars of the conservative cast of mind in education. All these thinkers are advocates of discipline, a word which seems to have fallen into disfavor among us nowadays. Discipline means, however, not mere meaningless adherence to routine, but order, the ordering of mind, the discovery of the elements in personality and in intellect that give purpose and coherence to life; and that is what the cultural conservative seeks.

It has become the fashion in many quarters nowadays to talk as if we live in unique times and ought to solve all of our present problems in terms of the moment. The cultural conservative contends that liberal education necessarily is traditional, that it is intended to conserve the heritage of our civilization. He maintains that this is a great, indeed a sacred, task: to guard and extend the body of known truth; in short, to preserve through intellectual and moral disciplines that great continuity and essence which we call culture.

Answers to Objections

Isn't conservative education undemocratic? Isn't it based on the idea of a privileged elite?

If I may venture briefly into autobiography, I don't think that is so —in my own experience. My father is a railroad engineer, that is, an engine driver, and my boyhood may be said to have been spent in the railroad yards; but I still had the privilege of reading Plutarch and

Samuel Johnson. We were, indeed, a book-reading family. This great cultural heritage of ours, which is maintained through the traditional disciplines, is not simply to benefit one class. It benefits all classes. The improvement of the mind is a universal opportunity. I don't see that good education is a matter of stratifying class lines. In truth, this generally-available disciplined instruction makes social mobility easier, enabling classes to have a common interest and persons to pass from class to class.

I think there is much nonsense talked about an elite. The word elite is not one that I particularly like; and T. S. Eliot also dislikes that term. We both prefer the term aristocracy. This, too, has come into some disrepute, but it is badly misunderstood. The American theory of equality is founded on the ancient idea of equality before the law and on the Christian idea of the brotherhood of all men in Christ. No able American has ever seriously maintained that all human beings are equal in intelligence or character; and the intelligent conservative believes that any educational system that is blind to the differences in intellect and aptitude among the rising generation must end in catastrophic failure. As Mr. David Riesman said recently, "Men are not born equal. They are born different." Although traditional education tries to give certain common basic disciplines to everyone in society, it also recognizes the natural, inescapable fact that we must train some minds for honorable and intelligent leadership, especially in a democracy.

Doesn't a philosophy that looks backward and seeks to preserve what has happened before tend to continue existing injustices and make it difficult or impossible to solve the social problems that face us?

That is the argument of the congenital radical who tends to look on the past somehow as evil in itself. That argument is especially favored by the Marxists, who maintain that we should sweep away the medieval or so-called feudal past and march on to a glorious people's paradise.

I think that is a profound error. It has been said that traditional education serves vested interests. I do not think it really does anything of the sort. True, traditional education does establish order and a sense of tranquility and harmony in society. This is really a benefit to everyone—to those favored with the goods of fortune, in Burke's phrase, and to those who are obscure and poor. Order is always preferable to anarchy; and there are two kinds of order: the inner order of the personality or the soul, and the outer order, the order of society. These, traditional education does try to preserve and improve. Conservative educators have always been especially interested in real justice as contrasted with the extravagant ideas of justice popular among the doctrinaire radicals. Plato, for instance, was primarily concerned with the idea of justice, and most conservative educators have been strongly influenced by Plato. The Marxist believes that the intellectual should be gnawing forever at the foundations of society. The conservative thinks otherwise; he believes that orderly society is a great good, that civilized life itself is good, and we ought to guard it and extend its blessings.

Isn't this effort to preserve the past antithetical to progress?

When I hear the term "progress" mentioned in connection with education, I think of a true anecdote related to me by Dr. Stanley Pargellis, now the director of the Newberry Library in Chicago and formerly Professor of History at Yale. When Dr. Pargellis was at Yale, a young graduate student came to him and said, "Sir, I want to get a Doctor's degree in history, and I want you to supervise my thesis." Dr. Pargellis asked, "What do you want to work on?" The young man said, "Why, I am interested in Progress," and he spoke as if it had a capital "P." "I know that history is a record of Progress. I know we are constantly getting better, and I mean to develop a thesis that will show how all history is a record of human Progress, with man escaping from superstition, poverty, sickness, and so forth, marching always onward." He looked up brightly, expecting to be clapped on the back. "Well, sir," said Dr. Pargellis, "suppose you should study history only to discover that there is no such thing as Progress. What would you do then?" "Why," said the young man, "What *could* I do? What would there be left to believe in?" "Then," said Dr. Pargellis, "you had best not become a doctor of philosophy in history."

Of course Dr. Pargellis' moral is not that no progress exists. There is progress with a small "p"; improvement in many things is possible and highly desirable, but the conservative educator knows progress is not inevitable. There are different kinds of progress. If, for instance, you find yourself progressing toward the edge of the cliff, it will be prudent to retrace your steps; and often mankind is in just this situation—progressing toward a cliff. The only kind of real knowledge possible is the knowledge of the past. The present is always slipping away from us; the future is unknowable. Therefore it is to the wisdom of our ancestors, to the traditional disciplines, to the great accumulated body of opinions, that we have to turn if we hope to keep back from that cliff edge.

An Example for Illustration and Comment

(The headmaster of a private military boys' school explains some of the aspects of the school life.)

"One of the major objectives of this academy is to provide boys with intellectual stimulation and to encourage them in scholarly pursuits. The library is an important resource in fulfilling these aims. Here the boys become familiar with the treasures of our written tradition and gain skill and discrimination in using them. But other pursuits also contribute to the development of individual ability.

Participation in sports teaches boys to work effectively with their fellows and to acquire such qualities as courage, self reliance, respect for others, and the ideals that go into the making of strong character. The curriculum includes strong offerings in the basic traditions of Western Civilization, including classical language and literature. The study of Latin gives the boys an idea of some of the sources of our own cultural and linguistic heritage. We also have a modern language laboratory. Some of our graduates will assume positions of leadership in government, diplomacy, and business where the ability to speak a foreign tongue fluently will be essential.

This academy includes military discipline as part of its program—in the conviction that ready obedience to properly constituted authority is a significant element in the development of mature manhood. Furthermore, preparation for responsible citizenship in modern society demands thorough grounding in the basic sciences, for which extensive laboratory experience is provided. The arts, too, belong to the great traditions of our society. Some of the boys achieve a memorable dramatic experience through participation in the production of plays by Shakespeare and other great dramatists. The academy boys have the privilege of expert instruction in small classes. For example, we have a senior seminar in government, which will help to prepare the boys to serve as intelligent leaders in civic and national enterprises."

This illustration represents very well what the traditionalist, the advocate of cultural conservation, desires in both method and aim of instruction. It is evidently the belief of the school that intellectual, moral, and other disciplines should be blended to produce a harmonious mind and personality. Persons unacquainted with an academy like this may feel that school uniforms, rifle drill, and athletics are unnecessary frills. They may not be absolutely essential to good instruction; but they are a part of the respect for order which is important to traditional instruction. You recall the remark of the Duke of Wellington that the Battle of Waterloo was won on the playing fields of Eton. Wellington said that in old age. As a matter of fact, it has been ascertained that while he himself was at Eton, Wellington played only croquet. So I don't know that the important part of this education is athletics, rifle drill, or uniforms. Most important of all is the instruction in traditional intellectual and moral disciplines obtained in the class in Latin, in the study of the great plays, in the study of government and politics, and in the work in the library which was previously described. Those indeed preserve the wisdom of our ancestors.

Concluding Suggestions

I say first of all that we require attention in primary and secondary schools to the studies that teach us what makes life worth living, and what are the possibilities and the limitations of human nature. Those studies are great literature; ancient and modern rhetoric; ancient, modern, and American history; and the true scientific disciplines. These are of first importance, and it is also important, whatever the difficulties may be in public schools, that there should be sound instruction in religion and in ethics.

Second, we need the restoration of a hierarchy of intellectual disciplines in our colleges and universities. What has been called by Mr. Jerome Ellison the "second curriculum" on the campus—the fun fair which overshadows learning, the frill and snap courses designed to attract lazy minds—must yield precedence to real training of the mind in our disorderly age. Mr. T. S. Eliot fears that in the future, as things are going, the nomads of the future will camp in their mechanized caravans upon the ruins of our ancient edifices. That can still be prevented, but it cannot be prevented unless we share and transmit the splendid inheritance of three thousand years of civilization. Unless we will do this, we will find ourselves living in a mechanized barbarism or, quite possibly, dying in the wreck of a civilization which has mistaken dollars and gadgets for virtue and wisdom.

CHAPTER 11 • A Reconstructionist View of Education

Theodore Brameld

• Since before the dawn of civilization, human beings have been engaged in a ceaseless struggle to improve themselves. Man seems endowed with a restlessness that drives him always to higher levels, a dissatisfaction with things as they have been and are, and a creative urge for improvement. Perhaps all of the achievements of civilization have come in response to the vision of prophets and seers. Every dynamic society has been shaken from complacency and routine by its reformers and critics. Reconstructionism as a philosophy of education belongs to this great tradition of protest, promise, and progress. Although it is historically related to the pragmatism of John Dewey and in many respects is allied to that view, reconstructionism possesses its own unique and novel features that grow out of profound reflection on the revolutionary events of recent decades. It is a philosophy that begins with the fact of rapid cultural change in our technological society and endeavors to show how through education this change can be responsibly directed.—EDITOR.

● *"While repudiating nothing of the constructive achievements of other educational theories, reconstructionism commits itself, first of all, to the renascence of modern culture. It is infused with a profound conviction that we are in the midst of a revolutionary period out of which should emerge nothing less than the control of the industrial system, of public services, and of cultural and natural resources by and for the common people who, throughout the ages, have struggled for a life of security, decency, and peace for themselves and their children.*

Education sufficiently dedicated to this purpose no longer remains, to be sure, on the fence of intellectual 'impartiality.' But it is an education which, for that very reason, is inspired with enthusiasm for research, for diffusion of knowledge, for humanly realized beauty, goodness, and truth—an education which, through the schools of America and of all other democracies, will at last demonstrate its capacity to play no longer a minor but a major role in the reconstruction of civilization." [11]

STATEMENT OF THE VIEWPOINT BY THEODORE BRAMELD

It is not easy to state the essentials of reconstructionism, particularly since this is an outlook very much in the process of formulating an adequate conception of what it means and what it is after; particularly, too, since as yet there aren't very many people who care to use this label to characterize the direction and the purposes that some of my associates and I have in mind when we use the term. Let me attempt, however, to suggest a few of many things that could be said about this emerging position.

Reconstructionism is an anthropological philosophy of education. As you know, anthropology is the science of culture, a very young science far from maturity. Yet, to look at education in the setting of culture and to see it as an agency for building, perpetuating, and modifying culture is to bring education back into the main course of human experience. I fear that we sometimes think of education in such an academic way that we divorce it from the central forces of culture. By placing philosophy of education in an anthropological context we may be able to provide it with a vitality and significance that it lacks when treated merely as an erudite, intellectual discipline.

From the many concepts that might be chosen to introduce an anthropological approach to education I select three. First, every culture known to man has *order*, by which I mean a structure or system. For instance, there are classes in all cultures. Or we can imagine concentric circles of group relationships beginning with the family and moving out toward wider and wider circles nationally and even internationally. Second, every culture has a *process*, that is, it has characteristic ways of change. Thus, it is dynamic, for there is no such thing as a really static culture. Third, every culture has *goals*, directions, and purposes that may not be entirely explicit to the members of the culture. If we look at education from this anthropological point of view, we see that, as an agency of culture, education also possesses order, processes, and goals.

Let me take one example of process from our contemporary situation. A great many students would agree that one of the basic process-characteristics of our time is that we are in a stage of world-wide crisis. True, all periods of culture, I suppose, have been involved in major or minor crises, but ours is in many ways today unique, both in scope and in quality. One of the many respects in which ours is unique is the fact that man's diabolical genius has now created the power to destroy himself overnight.

Some anthropologists would, I think, offer support to a philosophy of education that recognizes that we are living in an age of gigantic crisis. It is therefore one of the fundamental assumptions of reconstructionists that education has unprecedented tasks that would not exist in a more normal, less revolutionary or less dangerous time.

Next, consider an example from the anthropological concept of goals. Reconstructionism is, above all, a goal-centered, future-oriented philosophy of education. It is believed that man is a goal-seeking animal and that it is now possible, particularly with the aid of the human sciences such as anthropology, sociology, and psychology, to begin to delineate the fundamental goals of man—what he is groping for, what he wants in life—in a way that was not possible in earlier, less scientific times. If we ask the question, "What should be the goals of man?" the reconstructionist, again borrowing from anthropology and other human sciences, would say that there are at least two fundamental goals. First, there is the goal of a world-wide democracy, or a series of democracies. (Here democracy means the kind of social order where men are in control of their own destiny.) It is a goal that we have not begun to achieve across much of the earth. Moreover, this democracy or these democracies should be societies in which basic natural and human resources are under the control of the majority of the people, with their policies constantly subject to minority criticism and correction. Second, those of us who are willing to call ourselves reconstructionists are committed to the goal of a world government with authority to enforce its mandates. Reconstructionism is an internationally minded educational theory.

The crucial problems of political, economic, religious, aesthetic, and educational life should be brought into the center of the curriculum and not left on the periphery. I readily agree that this kind of education would be difficult, because the problems of building a world government, of creating democracies across the surface of the earth, are the toughest of all human problems. For their solution we need the utmost intellectual, as well as social, economic, and political power. The kind of education the reconstructionist wants thus enters into the lifestream of the culture, discarding if necessary any elements of the curriculum that do not contribute to the supreme task of education—to reconstruct the culture before the culture destroys itself.

Lastly, let us return to the first of the three great cultural categories. Order is a broad concept that ties together and encompasses the concepts of process and goals. Cultural order promises to give us, if you will, a new world view provided, not by speculation or by metaphysics, but by the sciences of man.

Answers to Objections

Does not social planning of the kind reconstructionists recommend destroy democratic individuality and freedom? How is this position consistent with the belief that in a democracy the people should determine their own destiny?

Consider for a moment the concept of order that I have only briefly touched on. It is perfectly true that cultural order is not necessarily, indeed it usually has not been, democratic. It has been a superimposed kind of order. The Middle Ages are a good example—a hierarchical order directed from the top down. But certainly it does not follow that, because many kinds of cultural order in history have been hierarchical or autocratic, they need to be. What the reconstructionist is aiming at, along with many others who do not call themselves by this name, is the kind or order created by people planning and thinking and reaching decisions together—from the bottom up rather than from the top down. This is the democratic way. I see no incompatibility whatsoever between planning and democracy, provided that planning is carried on through public processes of inquiry, criticism, and decision making.

There are many who believe teachers are in a sense outside the ongoing stream of life of a society. If this is so, does it make sense to propose that teachers should be given the opportunity to change the cultural order?

It is true that teachers, to a great extent, are outside the main stream. This is unfortunate; they should not be, and we want to bring them back in again. Teachers are citizens with the same rights and responsibilities as any one else. If they are to play their part, however, we are going to need, for one thing, a reinvigorated and reorganized teacher training program.

I do not for a moment doubt that education can play a major role in the remaking of culture. Indeed, if we look at the role that education has played in the history of cultures, it is simply not scientifically or historically correct to contend that education has been or is merely a transmitting process. Both formally and informally, it has also been a recreative process. "Man makes himself," says Childe, one of the great archeologists of the twentieth century, and this is the conception of education that reconstructionists advocate—an education in which teachers, students, and parents are involved in the vital tasks of community making and remaking. I see no incompatibility between the transmitting role and the recreative role for education. The trouble is that throughout most of the history of our nation it has performed primarily the transmitting function. We need to have it perform the recreative function also.

Isn't the reconstructionist unrealistic about human nature? Is there any reason to believe that changing the cultural pattern will solve any of the basic problems which each of us faces and which are rooted in our natures?

There is no simple black-and-white answer to this question. I find support among anthropologists and other social scientists who take the view that the redirection of human life has to come from both the outside and the inside. Of course personalities must be changed, too, and the role of the psychological sciences is fundamental to this job. But while we have to change human beings from the inside out, we also must change them from the outside in. The process is reciprocal and interactive. However, education has been particularly weak with respect to the latter of these two requirements, that is, the cultural process of changing from the outside in. If I may put it in a different way, education has been too psychology-centered and not enough anthropology-centered.

In this world where changes are occurring so rapidly and are causing great insecurity, you are advocating that we make still further changes. Should we not rather advocate an educational program that would bring stability?

Of course we need stability. There are certain constancies in life and in human nature that need to be preserved. Here I respect the conservative view of education. But just because some of our great traditions—for example, the Bill of Rights—deserve preservation, it does not follow that reinforcement of traditional patterns of life and culture is the chief task of the school.

Consider again the fact that we are deep in an age of crisis and that old ways of solving problems on the economic, the political, even the religious and the aesthetic levels, are no longer adequate to many of us. Consequently, while it isn't a matter of either/or—either conservation or change—reconstructionists take the view that the great role of the school now ought to be that of promoting purposeful, goal-directed changes toward the objectives suggested earlier—toward the creation of democracies throughout the world embracing all races, all creeds, all classes, and the establishment of world government. Such changes are fundamental to the preservation of civilization, and education, first of all, needs to be dedicated to the struggle for their attainment.

An Example for Illustration and Comment

(A social studies teacher speaks at a parents' night meeting, as follows:)

"Good evening, Ladies and Gentlemen. I have been asked to speak to you this evening about 'What your children will be learning this year in their social studies.' As I see it, one of the basic obligations of the teaching profession is to teach young people how to think. As you all will agree, this is rather difficult to do. In our social studies classes we go one step further. We give them something to think about and then we also help them to think constructively about it. For example, they are faced with the problems we had in our youth, but we try to give them some examples and to help them think constructively along new lines and perhaps come across better solutions.

Specifically, these are some of the topics we hope to cover this year: The Importance of Proper Use and Conservation of Our National Resources; The Problems Involved in Our Exploding World Population; and The Universal Elimination of Capital Punishment. The students will do a comparative study of cooperatives as they exist in the Scandinavian countries, in Israel, and (to a greater extent than most of us realize) in our own country. They will also do a study unit on World Government in which they will take up such forerunners of World Government as The United Nations, The World Bank, The World Court, and so forth. In closing, I would like to leave you with one basic thought. It is my hope each year as I work with the new students in my classes that a few will develop the leadership qualities that will enable them to set the pattern of continued and evolving growth in our social structure."

In some ways, I approve of what this teacher said. The fact that she was attempting to let the parents in on what she was doing, and seeking their support was commendable. I also liked the kind of questions she intended to raise with her students. These questions aren't discussed nearly enough in the average public school in the United States, or for that matter in the schools of many other countries.

But I am not entirely happy with what might have been an implication that these questions were simply going to be introduced into the conventional curriculum. We ought to go much further than that. There is an urgent need for new experimental types of curriculum, especially on the high school level, that would move far beyond the recent proposals of educators such as Dr. Conant. In these new types of curriculum, the *central* problems should be those of cultural reconstruction. For example, instead of studying world government, say one week in the year, or having one assembly period devoted to the United Nations, there ought to be at least one full semester, if not a full year, centering in problems of international order—the obstacles to achieving it as well as possible ways of moving toward it—based on completely realistic analyses of the world situation. Moreover, the sciences, the arts, and all others aspects of the curriculum should be integrated in terms of the basic problems of cultural reconstruction. And this means nothing less than a redesigned curriculum from top to bottom.

Concluding Suggestions

A primary need today is much more thorough communication between parents and other citizens and the school itself. A two-way traffic is absolutely essential if the schools are going to move ahead with the rapid pace that now seems essential.

Meanwhile, the schools themselves, with the support and understanding of parents, ought to break more new ground than they do with experiments and exploratory projects that do not require a wholly reorganized curriculum. And this applies not only in the field of the social studies, but in the natural sciences and in the arts. These projects and experiments may sometimes be mistaken, and may even fail, but from them as much may often be learned as from those that succeed.

Then there is need on the part of teachers for much stronger commitment to the enormous cultural potentialities of education. It is not, I think, an exaggeration to say that teaching is the greatest of all professions. Teachers ought to have a deep sense of adventure, of participation in an enterprise with high purpose and great goals. If teachers can acquire this attitude, they can become reconstructionist in spirit even though in practice it may be difficult for them to translate theory into practice quickly.

Finally, may I make a plea for the practical necessity of theory itself? It is no contradiction to say that there are times when the most practical thing a teacher or any other student of education can do is to become theoretical. The need for theoretical study of educational issues by teachers and by parents is imperative if we are to build strong education in the United States and in the world.

CHAPTER 12 · Education for
National Survival

Harold W. Stoke

- All social and political analysts agree that a fundamental responsibility of government is the common
defense. No civilization can endure and no society
can prosper without security from attack by enemies. To provide such security, trained personnel
are necessary. Such training is one of the important
tasks of education in every society and in every age.
This is no new idea, for one of the classic statements
of it is to be found in Plato's description of the education of the guardians in his famous *Republic*.

American educational theory until recently has
largely neglected this ancient lesson, which has been
greatly reinforced by the recent developments of
modern nationalism and machine technology. Our
educators have concentrated on the development of
the good life and the good society with little regard
for the rise of forces that threaten to destroy them
both. The hot and cold wars of recent decades and
the rapid scientific advances of the Communist and
other totalitarian countries have finally awakened
many thoughtful people to the obligations of education for national survival.

Thus, what was once an educational objective for
a limited professional group in the population has
been transformed by modern scientific and political
developments into a comprehensive educational
principle.—EDITOR.

- *"The new nationalism assumes that under conditions of life today all
of the activities of our national life must be so conducted as to contribute to the strength of the nation, and to this principle education
is no exception. It has begun to dawn upon us that education is an
instrument of power on which national survival itself depends, and
this indisputable fact has imposed upon education and upon educators
a new obligation, superior to any other; namely, to keep the nation
strong. There would be little education, at least of any kind we now
think desirable, unless there is national survival; and if national survival
depends on education, it is easy to conclude that education must be
consciously enlisted to serve the national needs. The swift developments of recent years begin to make such a direct relationship between
education and national necessity appear not only natural and accept-
able, but inevitable. The view has never been more explicitly put
than in a recent statement by national educational leaders that 'our
children's minds are the nation's greatest resource.'"* [12]

STATEMENT OF THE VIEWPOINT BY HAROLD W. STOKE

The basic proposition is really very simple. It starts from the fact that our nation faces danger, not only to its freedom of action, but even to its survival. As long as such dangers and threats continue, we shall have to conduct our national life in such a way as to insure for ourselves as a free nation sufficient national strength to protect not only ourselves but also the nations which are dependent on us. Although this is not a situation we desire or choose, it is one we must face. Unless we can insure for ourselves sufficient military and political strength to survive as a nation, the other values we prize, such as education, freedom, and welfare, cannot remain. Somerset Maugham after watching the fall of France in 1941, remarked that the nation that prizes wealth more than freedom will lose not only its freedom but its wealth also. So the survival of all other values depends on the strength of the nation which can protect them.

Most of us agree to this proposition, so long as we talk about the production of steel or food or the stockpiling of copper; but somehow we shrink from it when we talk about the self-conscious enlistment of education as a part of our national defense. Yet the adequate defense of a nation today involves almost every aspect of life, and it would be strange indeed if education, which is the most nearly universal activity of the American people, could be omitted. Of course education cannot possibly be omitted, for in this age of technology, national strength is more dependent on a high level of educational achievement than on any other factor. It is merely because Americans have rarely thought of education as an instrument of power or as a part of our apparatus for national defense that we are reluctant to do so now. But our wealth of resources and our freedoms of choice will do us little good unless they can produce the people who can protect them. Military power these days depends on science, and thus on the development of scientists. Political power depends on knowledge—of languages, psychology, economics, and history—and thus on the development of scholars.

This explains why there has recently been a great growth of interest and concern on the part of the national government in education. Whatever is necessary for our national defense the national government must provide, and if this means that it must have mathematicians, scientists, engineers, and linguists, it must not leave their production to chance, any more than it can afford to leave to chance the production of steel, drugs, or missiles. This is why today so many of our political and educational leaders are calling for the revitalization of American education, are asking that we lift the level of our student efforts, that we provide more generous support for education at both the national and the local levels, and that we guide our efforts much more self-consciously toward the creation of national strength. It is this new educational necessity—a necessity which is thrust on us by the developments of a new technology and by the rapid rise of new and threatening forces in the world—that our nation now faces and that we must take steps to meet with adequate preparation.

Answers to Objections

Is it not true that the real significance of a nation or of a civilization lies not in its physical power but in its moral and spiritual values?

The possession of power is not in itself immoral. Whether a power is good or not depends on what use is made of it. I hope that the power which the United States has will always be used for virtuous and valid ends. Certainly there is no virtue in weakness *per se,* and I doubt very much that the American people would be willing to scrap their national defense and trust to the good will which exists in the world today to preserve us as a nation. Historically, I know of no nation which has found it advantageous to be weak in power, regardless of what its cultural attainments were.

Education for national survival may help to save our skins, but can it provide us with anything really worth living for?

Quite frankly, yes. While survival as the end in view may at first seem to be unattractive and negative in character, closer examination shows that today almost the whole range of the activities of a nation is involved in building national strength. This concern for strength actually serves not as a limitation, but as a stimulus, to virtually every aspect of our life. Consider, for example, how much science has benefited from the tremendous concentration of national interest in this field during the last few years. Or, again, consider the fact that today there are probably more people than ever before studying foreign languages in the United States, and studying them effectively, because of the new political interest which our nation has in these accomplishments. On the whole, I believe that there are great cultural benefits to be derived from our interest in national strength, in addition to the political and military advantages which accrue from it.

In the lop-sided curriculum which this philosophy would dictate, with all the emphasis on science, engineering, and language, what will happen to philosophy, history, art, and the other humanities?

In a sense, curricula are always lop-sided, because knowledge does not grow evenly. Our prevailing lop-sidedness, if it is to be called that, in the direction of scientific development, actually has a most liberalizing and stimulating effect on other fields of knowledge. The tremendous encouragement for science these days has lifted the horizons of all the social studies as well. For example, we cannot now talk about natural resources in the same light as we did only a few years ago, because of the redirection of our interest toward such problems as production, distribution, marketing, and economic growth, as a result of our concern for national strength.

How can freedom, on which American democracy is based, be preserved under a federally dominated system of education for national survival?

I do not regard the national government as the enemy of American freedom. The national government in fact has a highly commendable record of protecting individual freedom both at national and local levels. Anyway, if the choices before us are really those of national survival, how is individual freedom going to survive at all, unless the educational system contributes its part to the strength of the nation?

It would seem that education for national survival means that henceforth the Russians are going to call the tune for American education. Dare we project our national program of education on the basis of trying to keep up with Russia?

I deny this common charge, that the Russians today are calling the American educational tune. What is determining our current preoccupation is not the Russians, but the character of the new kinds of knowledge that have been released in the world. Regardless of whether the knowledge of how to split the atom or to get to the moon is in the hands of the Russians or the Chinese or the Americans, we have no choice but to pursue such knowledge ourselves.

An Example for Illustration and Comment

(Following is a statement about the new United States Air Force Academy at Colorado Springs:)

The United States Air Force Academy is a major tangible result of our government's official recognition that national survival depends on education.

Qualifications for entrance are high. Following recommendation by their congressmen, students must pass rigid physical fitness tests, Air Force qualifying tests, College Entrance Examination Board tests, and the Air Force medical examination for flying training.

Once the students are admitted, they follow a rigorous four-year program. There is much emphasis on physical training, plus basic training in scientific and liberal arts fields. At the same time, all students receive professional airmanship training.

Upon being graduated, each student receives a Bachelor of Science degree, a commission as second lieutenant in the Air Force, and the aeronautical rating of navigator. Those physically qualified go on after graduation for a complete course in pilot training.

Probably for all of us, air science illustrates the dramatic climax of modern technology. Currently it is our most dramatic as well as our most effective reliance for national defense. To fly a plane or to create a missile requires some of the most complex scientific knowledge we now possess. It involves mathematics, physics, engineering, metallurgy, and meteorology. In fact almost every aspect of modern scientific knowledge is now combined in the kinds of activities illustrated by the preceding example.

However, the changes in technology today are so rapid and so startling that we have to be light on our feet. Today we are flying planes or directing missiles; tomorrow we may be manning satellites. Consequently, what we have achieved at any given time is never sufficient for the needs of national strength. The real requirement is constantly to increase our knowledge of the kind of universe in which we live. This is the burden we have assumed in accepting responsibilities for modern knowledge and for transforming it into practical applications for the strength of the nation. This is then the principal burden of education itself, and one which we must face realistically as a nation.

Concluding Suggestions

Changing the character or the trends of a national educational system is a difficult task, involving as it does the traditions, habits, and values of an immense number of people. Still there are some things I think we can do.

First, in a democratic society such as ours we must increase the general level of public appreciation of education as an indispensable factor in the development of national strength. This amazing society of ours, with all its capacity to produce goods and distribute services, was not built nor can it be maintained by ignoramuses. We shall need more people with more education not merely to sustain the level we now have achieved, but to increase that level and to develop the strength which our society must have.

Second, we must challenge our young people from the very outset with the limitless opportunities of knowledge these days. We must find ways of exposing them imaginatively to the opportunities and responsibilities they have in wisely applying the new kinds of knowledge.

Third, as a society, we must find ways of discovering our best talent and of seeing to it that this talent is developed to the highest possible degree through education. We can do this through scholarship and loan programs, but even more through the schools' identification and encouragement of the bright minds which can be turned in specialized directions.

Finally, we must be willing to spend a larger proportion of our national income on education. Although America already spends large amounts on education, we are a very wealthy nation, and many other countries spend a larger proportion of their national income on this most vital of all activities.

CHAPTER 13 · Education for Freedom

R. Freeman Butts

- Freedom is one of the perennial goals of human civilization and one of the primary measures for gauging cultural progress. As such, it has been an important goal of education. The citizens of the city-states of ancient Greece were taught the discipline of free men. Stoicism in Roman civilization was concerned with making men inwardly free. Jews and Christians through the centuries have sought to impart the truth in order that men might be liberated from the bondage of sin and ignorance. The scientific progress of the past four hundred years has been based on the ideal of the freedom of inquiry.

  Modern history has been marked by the growing recognition that liberty belongs not to a privileged class but to all men. Most of the social revolutions and reformations of recent centuries have sought to expand political, economic, religious, and personal freedom. In these movements, education has played an important part.—EDITOR.

- *"Popular education is necessary for the preservation of those conditions of freedom, political and social, which are indispensable to free individual development. No instrumentality less universal in its power and authority than government can secure popular education. In order to secure popular education the action of society as a whole is necessary; and popular education is indispensable to that equalization of the conditions of personal development which are the proper object of society. Without popular education, moreover, no government which rests upon popular action can long endure; the people must be schooled in the knowledge, and if possible in the virtues, upon which the maintenance and success of free institutions depend. No free government can last in health if it lose hold of the traditions of its history, and in the public schools these traditions may be and should be sedulously preserved, carefully replanted in the thought and consciousness of each successive generation."* [13]

STATEMENT OF THE VIEWPOINT BY R. FREEMAN BUTTS

The preceding quotation from Woodrow Wilson emphasizes that the freedom of the individual is related to the conditions of the society in which the individual lives. Freedom is double-barreled. We can- not have free individuals without a free society and we cannot have a free society without free individuals. Wilson's statement is certainly in the American tradition of freedom and education.

When we think of freedom in its most common sense, we usually mean "freedom *from*"—the condition of being free from constraint and obstacles, of doing what one wishes. But there are two other meanings that are equally important, namely, "freedom *of*"—freedom of thought, of religion, of speech, and of press—and, "freedom *to*"—the opportunity to make choices, to make decisions, and to act on those choices. I like to think of the free person as one who is politically, intellectually, and personally free. We need a society that cultivates and nourishes these three freedoms. Thus, the right, the opportunity, and the ability to make choices and to carry out these choices, seem to me to be the essence of freedom.

We need an education that deliberately tries to cultivate these three kinds of freedom. Notice that I have not mentioned "freedom *for*." This is where education comes in. I do not believe that any society or group of people should decide for a person what his freedom is for. This makes particularly important the kind of education that will enable a person to make desirable decisions for himself. Therefore it seems to me that education must concentrate on three elements. First, we need knowledge, the broadest range of knowledge now available to mankind. No person can be free today without a genuine understanding, insofar as it is possible to get it, of the kinds of knowl- edge represented by our humanities and arts, by the social sciences, and by the natural sciences and mathematics. My late colleague, Lyman Bryson, pointed out that for our own safety, we must be able to distinguish between the significant truth, the plausible falsehood, and the beguiling half-truth. Intellectual freedom requires this kind of ability to discriminate second-rate from first-rate knowledge. Second, we need education for citizenship, for social responsibilities. We have long felt that our schools should do this, and now we must be at this job even more strenuously and intelligently than before. Thirdly, we need emphasis on personal freedom to help individuals to develop their own peculiar talents. The real goal of freedom is self-fulfillment, not just happiness in any small sense.

In order to organize education for freedom, there are several principles that I believe are necessary in a society like ours. First, we must recognize that the free people through their free government have the right and the obligation to provide public education, free for everyone, supported by all, and available freely to everyone. I like to think of public education as a kind of fourth branch of government, really as important for the nourishment of a free society as the executive, the legislative, and the judicial branches.

Second, there must be freedom for private schools and colleges, and freedom for parents to send their children to these private institutions. The states have no right to abolish or damage private schools, but similarly, they have no right to abolish or damage their own public schools. Both kinds of schools must be available.

Third, I believe in our tradition that public funds raised by taxation of all should go to the public schools, rather than to the private schools. Education is certainly of benefit to individuals, but its claim on public funds arises from its contribution to the public good. I agree with Woodrow Wilson, that free education is the chief regenerative agency of a free society.

Fourth, although the states have a broad authority over education, both public and private, in our tradition, we as a people have decided that it is best for the states to delegate to local school boards and professional staffs the day-to-day management of the schools.

Fifth and last, for genuine freedom, it seems to me that the federal government, while it does not widely operate or manage schools directly, does have the right to lay down the laws and principles of liberty and equality under which the school systems themselves must operate.

In summary, a free education is a necessity for the nourishment of free individuals in a free society.

Answers to Objections

National and international problems being what they are, do we not need federal control of education, rather than local control, as you recommend?

No, I do not think we need direct federal control of education. The control of education in America is divided among local, state, and federal levels of government. We have certain broad national policies, but these need to be carried out at the local level. I think our variety of controls under a common national policy is perhaps the best arrangement. Freedom is not a matter of allowing anyone to do anything he wishes, nor is it a matter of imposing measures upon local groups without opportunity for them to take part. There are, however, certain basic principles of liberty and equality which we as a whole people have decided on and which are contained in our Constitution and in our legal and political traditions. It seems to me that local majorities may not violate these any more than national majorities may.

With public schools subject to political control, are not the private schools the only places that educational freedom can be preserved?

Parents do have a basic choice, whether to send their children to private or to public schools. But notice the term "public schools." In America we use this term, rather than "state schools" or "government schools," which are the terms commonly used in other countries. I think these usages are correct. Our schools are "public" in the sense that they are really controlled by the people, in three different ways: through boards of education, elected or appointed by the people; through state government, responsible to the people; and through federal government, also responsible to the people.

Furthermore, the professional staffs, appointed at the local level, by having common professional and scholarly standards, give a broad, common outlook to our schools. Their freedom is exercised within the framework of loyalty to the canons of scholarship and knowledge. The profession must have a certain autonomy and freedom in public schools, as well as in private schools. Then the public through its voluntary organizations may make known its ideas and its claims on the public authorities in charge of education, and the profession may respond to these claims and in turn try to exert leadership in the interest of scholarship and of knowledge.

Have not our public schools tended to make all of us more or less alike, creating a vast and drab mediocrity? Can education make people of average ability wise enough to govern themselves?

I think it not only can, but it has and it must. James Madison once said something like this: "Knowledge must always win over ignorance, and a people who would be their own governors must have knowledge." If we have any faith in the democratic process, *everyone* must have the opportunity to develop himself through education to the highest level possible. All of our history shows that the rise in level of sheer economic ability and of political maturity has to do with the fact that very early we established a free system of universal education.

As for the problem of mass conformity, although it is true that freedom can be destroyed by an arbitrary government, a tyrannical majority, or a despotic minority, I believe that in our society the pressure to conform comes from the industrial and commercial elements in their effort to make people alike. Actually, our schools, both public and private, have probably given people more opportunity to be themselves than have schools anywhere else in the world.

An Example for Illustration and Comment

In 1952, in the case of Wieman *versus* Updegraf, the Supreme Court of the United States unanimously held invalid a state statute which prescribed loyalty oaths for certain public officers and employees, including teachers, as being in conflict with the due process clause of the Fourteenth Amendment to the federal Constitution.

The following statement from Justice Frankfurter's concurring opinion bears on the issue of academic freedom:

"Public opinion is the ultimate reliance of our society only if it be disciplined and responsible. It can be disciplined and responsible only if habits of open-mindedness and of critical inquiry are acquired in the formative years of our citizens. The process of education has naturally enough been the basis of hope for the perdurance of our democracy on the part of all our great leaders, from Thomas Jefferson onwards.

To regard teachers— . . . from the primary grades to the university— as the priests of our democracy is therefore not to indulge in hyperbole. It is the special task of teachers to foster those habits of open-mindedness and critical inquiry which alone make for responsible citizens, who, in turn, make possible an enlightened and effective public opinion. Teachers must fulfill their function by precept and practice, by the very atmosphere which they generate; they must be exemplars of open-mindedness and free inquiry. They cannot carry out their great and noble task if the conditions for the practice of a responsible and critical mind are denied to them. They must have the freedom of responsible inquiry, by thought and action, into the meaning of social and economic ideas, into the checkered history of social and economic dogma. They must be free to sift evanescent doctrine, qualified by time and circumstance, from that restless, enduring process of extending the bounds of understanding and wisdom, to assure which the freedoms of thought, of speech, of inquiry, of worship are guaranteed by the Constitution of the United States against infraction by national or state government."

That is an excellent statement with which I agree fully. I would simply re-emphasize the point that the loyalty oath requirement is really an attack on freedom of the mind. I said earlier that persons must be free to make conscious choices between real alternatives. Thus any attempt to rule out beliefs is to that degree an infringement and a constraint on freedom of belief. The essence of freedom in education is to enable the mind to range widely and to reach its own conclusions. We may, of course, need to limit freedom of action, but in a free society we should not try to limit freedom of belief.

The objection to government interference in the affairs of schools and colleges is also important. I would point out, however, that in a free society, governments may guarantee freedom and equality and may promote them as well as infringe them. Thus, for example, the desegregation decision of the federal government requires that the states not discriminate against children on the basis of race in the public schools.

Concluding Suggestions

I would urge citizens to work diligently to get the schools to adopt and use the very best resources of modern scholarship. I would urge teachers to range widely and freely, opposing all restrictions on learning and teaching. I would urge teachers and school administrators to be critical and outspoken. After all, the free society is the only society that delegates to its educational system this task of criticizing itself. I would urge parents and citizens generally to support the ideal of education for public service rather than for private consumption and private interests. One of the best ways for citizens to improve education is to work in and through the public school systems. I would urge citizens to encourage the educational profession to strengthen itself by greater devotion to scholarship and to professional ideals. Finally, I would urge all citizens to work zealously to increase the financial support for education, which is the fundamental bulwark of our freedom.

· Biographical Notes

ARTHUR BESTOR is Professor of History at the University of Illinois. He was educated at Yale University and also holds a degree from Oxford. He has taught history at Yale University, Teachers College Columbia University, Stanford University, the University of Wisconsin, and Oxford University, where he served as Harmsworth Professor of American History. He is author of numerous articles on history and on education and, among others, of the following books: *The Restoration of Learning, Educational Wastelands,* and *Education and Reform at New Harmony.*

EUGENE B. BOROWITZ is national director of education for the Union of American Hebrew Congregations. He is a graduate of the Ohio State University and holds Doctor's degrees from Hebrew Union College and Columbia University. After being ordained in 1948, Dr. Borowitz served as Rabbi of congregations in St. Louis, Missouri and Port Washington, New York. He is the author of numerous articles and monographs in the field of Jewish education.

THEODORE BRAMELD is Professor of Educational Philosophy at Boston University. He was educated at Ripon College and the University of Chicago. He taught at Long Island University, Adelphi College, Dartmouth College, Columbia, Wisconsin, Minnesota, and New York Universities, the University of Puerto Rico, the New School for Social Research, and the William Alanson White Institute of Psychiatry before taking his present post. He has been active in the Progressive Education movement, and in other educational and scholarly societies. He is past president of the Philosophy of Education Society. Among his books are *Education for the Emerging Age, Philosophies of Education in Cultural Perspective,* and *Toward a Reconstructed Philosophy of Education.*

HARRY S. BROUDY is Professor of Education at the University of Illinois, where he teaches in the field of Philosophy of Education. He was educated as an undergraduate at the Massachusetts Institute of Technology and at Boston University. He earned his Ph.D. in Philosophy at Harvard University. For twenty years he served on the faculties of the Massachusetts State Teachers Colleges at Framingham and at North Adams. He is past president of the Philosophy of Education Society, author of *Building a*

Philosophy of Education, and co-author of *Psychology for General Education.*

R. FREEMAN BUTTS is William F. Russell Professor in the Foundations of Education at Teachers College, Columbia University. He received his education at the University of Wisconsin, and for the past twenty-five years has been on the faculty at Teachers College. His present chair was created especially for the purpose of promoting the study of freedom and education. Among the books of which Professor Butts is the author are *The College Charts its Course, A Cultural History of Western Education, The American Tradition in Religion and Education,* and *A History of Education in American Culture.* Recently he has written for the National Education Association *Journal* a brief story of American education under the title, *The Search for Freedom.*

MERRIMON CUNINGGIM is Director of the Danforth Foundation of St. Louis. He was educated at Vanderbilt and Duke Universities, studied as a Rhodes Scholar at Oxford University, and took his theological and doctoral work at Yale University. He has served as Director of Religious Activities at Duke University and on the faculties of Denison University and Pomona College in the field of religion. For nine years prior to taking his present post he was Dean of the Perkins School of Theology at Southern Methodist University. He is the author of several books on religion and education, including *The College Seeks Religion* and *Freedom's Holy Light.*

ROBERT J. HENLE, a member of the Jesuit order, is Professor of Philosophy and Dean of the Graduate School at St. Louis University. He received his bachelor's and master's degrees at St. Louis University and his Ph.D. at the University of Toronto. Among his published works are *Saint Thomas and Platonism* and *Method in Metaphysics.* Father Henle is a past president of the Philosophy of Education Society.

H. GORDON HULLFISH is Professor of Education at the Ohio State University, where he has served on the faculty since 1922. He took his undergraduate degree at the University of Illinois and his graduate work at the university where he now serves. He has been a visiting professor at leading universities in this country and abroad. He has been president of the Philosophy of Education Society and of the John Dewey Society. He has written extensively in the field of educational philosophy, and is co-author of *Democracy in the Administration of Higher Education* and *Reflective Thinking.*

ARTHUR T. JERSILD is Professor of Education at Teachers College, Columbia University, in the Department of Psychological Foundations and Services. He was educated at the University of Nebraska and at Columbia University. He has taught psychology at the University of Nebraska, at the University of Wisconsin, and at Barnard College in addition to his service at Teachers College, where he has taught for the past thirty years. His books include

In Search of Self, Psychology of Adolescence, and *Child Psychology,* the last of which is now in its fifth edition.

RUSSELL KIRK is editor of *The University Bookman,* lecturer and essayist on historical, political, sociological, and philosophical subjects, short story writer, and research professor of political science at C. W. Post College, Long Island University. He was educated at Michigan State and Duke Universities, and at St. Andrews University in Scotland. Among his many books are *The Conservative Mind, A Program for Conservatives,* and *Academic Freedom.* He has also written critical introductions for sixteen volumes in the Gateway series of scholarly reprints.

ERNEST M. LIGON is Professor of Psychology at Union College, Schenectady, New York, and Director of the Character Research Project, which he founded at Union College in 1935. He received his undergraduate education at Texas Christian University and did his graduate work at Yale University. Prior to assuming his present position he taught at Yale University and at Connecticut College. Dr. Ligon has traveled and lectured widely on character education, working with experimental groups throughout the country in this field. He is the author of *The Psychology of Christian Personality, Their Future Is Now, A Greater Generation, Dimensions of Character,* and numerous other writings.

PHILIP H. PHENIX is Professor of Education in the Department of Social and Philosophical Foundations of Education, at Teachers College, Columbia University. He is a graduate of Princeton University and Union Theological Seminary in New York, and took his Ph.D. at Columbia University. He was formerly Dean of Carleton College, where he had earlier served as a member of the faculty. He is the author of *Intelligible Religion, Philosophy of Education,* and *Religious Concerns in Contemporary Education,* as well as numerous articles on religion and education.

HAROLD W. STOKE is President of Queens College in New York City. He was educated at Marion College, the University of Southern California, and the Johns Hopkins University. He has taught political science at several colleges and universities, has served as graduate dean at three institutions, and has been president of the University of New Hampshire and Louisiana State University in addition to his present post. Dr. Stoke has also been associated with our national life in several positions. He was connected with the Oak Ridge Nuclear Studies Development, he is a member of one of the commissions of the National Science Foundation, and he is United States representative on the governing committee of the Office of European Economic Cooperation. Among other books, he is author of *The Foreign Relations of the Federal State* and *The American College President.*

FLORENCE STRATEMEYER is Professor of Education in the Department of Curriculum and Teaching at Teachers College, Columbia University, where she has served on the faculty for thirty-six years, and where she also earlier received her higher education. She taught elementary school in Detroit for several years and also served as an assistant principal there. She has written extensively in the field of curriculum and on teacher education. Among the books of which she is one of the authors are *Developing a Curriculum for Modern Living, Teacher Education for a Free People, School and Community Laboratory Experiences in Teacher Education,* and *Working with Student Teachers.*

· References
for Quotations

1. John Dewey, *Democracy and Education*. New York: The Macmillan Company, 1915, pp. 320–322 *passim*.
2. John Wild, in *Modern Philosophies and Education*, Fifty-fourth Yearbook of the National Society for the Study of Education, edited by Henry Nelson. Part I. Chicago: The University of Chicago Press, 1955, p. 31.
3. Florence B. Stratemeyer, Hamden L. Forkner, Margaret McKim, and A. Harry Passow, *Developing a Curriculum for Modern Living*. New York: Bureau of Publications, Teachers College, Columbia University, 1957, Chapter V, *passim*.
4. Clifton Fadiman, in *The Case for Basic Education*, edited by James D. Koerner. Boston: Little, Brown & Company, 1959, pp. 5–6.
5. Arthur T. Jersild, *When Teachers Face Themselves*. New York: Bureau of Publications, Teachers College, Columbia University, 1956, *passim*.
6. George E. Partridge, *Genetic Philosophy of Education*. New York: The Macmillan Company, 1912, p. 167.
   Walter Scott Athearn, *Character Building in a Democracy*. New York: The Macmillan Company, 1924, p. 32.
   George A. Coe, *Education in Religion and Morals*. Chicago: Fleming Revell and Company, 1904, pp. 18–19.
7. Theodore M. Greene, "Religion and the Philosophies of Education," *Religious Education*. March–April 1954, pp. 82ff.
8. Pope Pius XI, in "Encyclical on the Christian Education of Youth," *Five Great Encyclicals*. New York: The Paulist Press, 1939, pp. 64–65.
9. From *The Living Talmud*, edited by Judah Goldin. New York: New American Library, 1958, p. 233.
10. William Bagley, *Education and Emergent Man*. New York: The Ronald Press Company, 1934, pp. 154–156.
11. Theodore Brameld, adapted from *Education for the Emerging Age*. New York: Harper and Brothers, 1961, pp. 26–27.
12. Harold W. Stoke, "National Necessity and Educational Policy," *Current Issues in Higher Education*. Washington: The Association for Higher Education, The National Education Association, 1959, p. 13.
13. Woodrow Wilson, *The State*. Boston: D. C. Heath Company, 1907, pp. 638–639.

All of the quotations are used by permission of the publishers indicated, to whom grateful acknowledgment is made.

INDEX